Healing for the Holes in Our Souls

Sharon L. Patterson

Sharon L. Patterson
A SCRIBE FOR ALL SEASONS

Beth,
May the Lord
bring keep that
call under
the places you
long to have
opened to my
this peace
understanding
healing

ISBN: 978-1535426169

Printed in the United States of America by CreateSpace

Library of Congress Control Number: 2008906705

Healing for the Holes in Our Souls

Dedication

This book is dedicated to those who have partnered with God to love, befriend, and minister to me throughout God's gracious healing in my life.

To my partner in marriage and life's journey:

Garry Patterson—thank you for healing patience, constant stability, and the unconditional love you have given me and our family these past twenty-six years. Every step of this book has your helping handprint all over it. Thank you, my incredible husband!

To my partners in ministry, healing, and enduring friendship:

Pat and Randall Jones—thank you for truth spoken in love, lasting loyalty, and faithful friendship. You have been there in every crisis and blessing. You have shared godly counsel, ministry, family times, road trips, and fun at the lake house. It has been a pleasure to serve with you in ministry and to share life together for over eighteen years.

To my pastors and leaders in ministry at Celebration Church:

Pastors Joe and Lori Champion—thank you for the renewed sense of Christian service you have inspired, and your encouragement to connect with God's destiny for this time of my life. I am so grateful for your delivery of God's truth through awesome preaching and teaching, and for walking out what you talk about. Your love and service to Jesus and Celebration Church is contagious!

Mel Stabber, LPC, and Pastoral Care Leader—thank you for your wise counsel, for the hours you have sacrificially spent reading, editing, and graciously writing the foreward of this manuscript. Bless you for all you do and for the care you give our church family.

To my partners in prayer, support, encouragement, and friendship:

Jo Clem—thank you for choosing me as your friend at thirteen! You shared your mom when mine was so ill. The memory of her peanut butter midnight snacks, lovingly prepared for two giggly teenage girls, sustained me through some difficult days! Thank you for remaining, for forty-seven years, my caring, truth-giving friend, and supportive Christian sister.

Karen Bennie—thank you for being my constant sounding board. You are a beautiful, trusted friend, and you have added incredible beauty and practical wisdom to my life. You are such a part of who I have become. You have been a true sister to me in every way possible throughout our thirty-six-year friendship.

Debbie Oliver—thank you for your continued prayers, constant support, awesome encouragement, and precious Christian friendship. Who could have guessed that a three-hour airplane ride from Chicago to Austin would lead to such a treasured relationship? You are my best cheerleader!

Joyce Williams, Sylvia Burgin, Henrietta Bean, Molly Metcalf, and Colleen Lucas—"*The Girls*"—thank each of you for giving me room to grow these past eighteen years, hugs that healed, counsel that worked, and fun that relaxed this strong Type-A personality. Your enduring friendship is a continual blessing!

Sharlyne Crisp—thank you for your Christian friendship, merciful heart, and consistently powerful intercessory prayer. Your prophetic words edified and ministered personally to my family and me. It has been a delight to team with you in the freedom ministry this past ten years.

Barbara Nedderman—thank you for the indispensable counsel that began as we pushed your baby daughter Emily in her stroller at the park near your home so many years ago. Thank you for encouraging me and editing my early writings. God has certainly blessed this three-decade-old friendship with His sustaining grace, enabling us to survive the broken places of heart and life.

Contents

Introduction

When I began to think about writing this book, a story from my childhood popped into my mind. My mother, a child of the Depression, relayed to me on more than one occasion the way she had to repair the holes in the soles of her only pair of Oxford shoes. Nightly, she would cut cardboard, paint the bottom of it with black shoe polish, and place it in the shoe to cover the hole so that she could wear them to school the next day. It was a constant care issue...trying to fill the hole and hide it.

As I thought about this story, I realized how similar a process we go through when we attempt to fill and hide the holes in our souls so that we can go into the public places of our lives. How meticulous we must be to fill those places with just the right thing so that no one can see the holes in the fabric of our soul—until the disguise breaks down. It always does because we use temporary materials to fill those holes. At that point, we must go to the soul-maker Himself. He alone possesses the right substance to permanently mend the holes in our souls.

So, my mother's story and my own led me to title this book as I have. As is often the case in Christian lay ministry, finding the healer of my soul spurred me to help others find Him, too. For twenty-five years, I have been involved with helping others find the great soul-mender, Jesus Christ.

With great faith in Him, I reach out to those seekers wishing to be filled with His light and His life. This invitation comes from the grateful heart of one who was once among the neediest of His children. I was a prime candidate for His healing touch. Now, I am a grown-up poster-child to the testimony of His work. Won't you join me? There is room on the poster!

With love, faith, and greatest blessing,

Sharon L. Patterson

foreward

God created us with many gifts and abilities. One such gift is the ability to establish internal thought patterns and/or external behaviors in difficult situations, allowing us to survive even the most heinous of events. As we live through crises, survival mechanisms protect us from destruction. Unfortunately, with those survival mechanisms in place, when we come into "greener pastures," we too often bring the behaviors or thoughts that served us in our survival into this new arena, causing us to behave in destructive ways. In fact, as one comes into the truth of God's Word, it becomes clear that those survival behaviors are actually contradictory to God's plan for our lives. Internal conflict stirs within the heart and soul concerning letting go those things that have served to protect us over the years and grasping a new way of thinking and behaving.

Most books of this nature come to us through the passive observations outsiders make while working with individuals on their journey towards healing or from a theological point of view that would dictate what God's Word says about the subject. Sharon Patterson's perspective comes from both points of view. She invites the reader into her world and makes herself vulnerable, bringing healing to those still wrestling with letting go of the old in order to embrace the new.

I find it refreshing to participate in the chronicles of someone who has served as both the healed and the healer. I invite readers to join her journey in the pages of *Healing for the Holes in Our Souls* and to allow God to use Sharon's life story to bring truth to your own situation, so that God can bring you to a new place of healing. He has brought you this far, and He wants to take you to the abundant life He promised.

Mel Stauber, LPC

Holes in Our Souls Are Common to Us All

*H*ere it is—the beginning, the first chapter—the start of another book. What piqued your interest as you picked up yet another "see-if-I-can-get-some-help" book, glanced at its title, flipped a few pages, and deemed it worth a trip to the checkout counter? Hopefully, it was the intent prayed over when it was written.

You may have already surmised that a professional psychiatrist or psychologist did not pen this book. You are so right. I stand in the same forever-long grocery lines, talk on the same call-dropping cell phones, and go to the same every-other-corner Starbucks, and order the same tall, no-whip mocha as you. (Oh, really? A grande caramel macchiato? I'll have to try that next time!)

My life, like yours, is full of normal activities set against the backdrop of everyday occurrences. There are unmeasured blessings and countless, ouchy boo-boos. (I am a grandmother of four-soon to be five.) Sidesplitting laughter and bottomless tears exist in close proximity to overwhelming joy and sorrow. Only hours separate triumphs and heart-numbing trials. Sometimes moments of fearless faith follow moments of anxiety's faithless fears. Other times, it is just the opposite.

We work and play together in life's front yards and backyards. There is always the familiar presence of glorious life and interrupting death, true saints and tainted sinners, endless wars and the persistent pursuit of peace, terrorist cowards, and medal-deserving heroes and heroines, voiceless victims and eloquent deliverers, and the wisdom of the political savvy as well as mindless chatter from the politically insane.

We see it all every single day, every hour on satellite or cable, on every channel. It is projected onto our wide-screen wall units or on the plasma television bought as much for size as technology. It may even come across on the plain old TV found at a garage sale, inherited from Aunt Lucy, won in a contest, or purchased at Sam's because of the ad in last Sunday's newspaper.

Speaking of Aunt Lucy and work, you and I even know some of the same people. Haven't we all worked for memorable bosses as well as those whose names you and I would just as soon forget? What about those incredible, life-long, faithful friends? Where would we be without them? (Daddy said we would be fortunate if we come through life with two!) I understand the other kind of friend, too. Just like you, I assumed they would be along for the whole journey and was devastated when they dropped out. Some even turned on me. You, too, huh?

Then, there is family. My, oh, my—what stories we could tell! Goodness, the characters we have met and shared meals and holidays with, voluntarily or involuntarily. Why, we may even be one of the characters our other family members talk about on the phone. Are there incriminating e-mails about you circling the four corners of the earth?

So, has life, its circumstances and relationships, given us something else in common? Absolutely! We share the results of what being in and belonging to this world has cost us—holes in our souls. Some holes are not our fault, and some holes are. Some are caused by trauma and some by people. The holes never seem to stop hurting; they are deep, and covered with self-protection. They are infected and infectious and need lancing, healing, and filling.

Lest I sound exhaustingly negative, let me interject hope with some wonderful news! Our holes are intended to be mended. They are not terminal tears unless we choose to ignore them. They require a doctor, a specialist among specialists—one that not only has studied holes, but also experienced them, one who knows us because He created us, came to earth, and walked as one of us.

With committed persistence, this Great Physician pursued my heart to submit to His expertise, that I might find much-needed healing. His remedy has been varied. Sometimes, He performed surgery with an instant miracle. More often than not, He sutured in people—people in my family and people missing from the family.

He used emotionally whole and emotionally distraught people. He used friends, and He used enemies. The common thread running through those He used? His two-fold requirement to yield in trust to His work through them and apply forgiveness. We will discuss this at length in a later chapter.

He sent me to palaces and playgrounds, foreign countries, and my own back yard. In familiar and unusual places, I have been helped equally by the highly degreed and the humble of heart. There is no perfect pattern of personality that determines who God chooses to help, nor is there a perfect person He chooses to empower to give help. He is not limited to place. He does, however, insist that it be according to His plan.

I chuckle to myself because for many of my sixty-plus years, I have tended to over-explain everything. It is the old-school teacher in me, I guess. As I felt compelled to deal with the subject of emotional healing, I found that I wanted to be uncomplicated, clear, and precise. It is my heart's desire that with the utmost simplicity, you, my fellow hole-in-the-soul companions, will be led to the doctor of absolute healing.

He is the soul-maker, the soul-keeper, and the soul-healer all in one. He is God, who walked as a man on this earth. He knows us best. There is no soul whose wounding He has not observed. He can see straight through our talk to our heart's motivations, whether we see ourselves as a Genghis Khan or a Mother Teresa inside. Although He is aware of the holes in our souls, He loves us unconditionally. He came to offer us His divine healing. I am so very glad He did because when I became aware of the holes in my soul, I called upon His Name and His services.

He is some doctor: He charges no fees, makes house calls at any hour of the day or night, and is not moved by how many holes need tending, or how loudly I protest the pain or process of healing. Upon invitation, He lovingly and thoroughly cleans each wounded place, patiently applies proper medication, and carefully checks the progress. He even provides a full-time caretaker as He heals—The Holy Spirit. He leads me to others in His service when I get stuck in some part of the healing process. Now, wouldn't you want to get this doctor's name and find out how to get to see Him?

It isn't always that simple, is it? Sometimes it is easier to continue with the holes in our souls. After all, no one is perfect. Everyone has holes. Why should we look where we don't want? "My holes are too deep," we protest. "Leave well enough alone. Let sleeping dogs lie! Don't go digging up old bones! I may be in pain, but at least it is familiar!"

Ah, familiarity, the great preference, and at times, the greatest enemy of healing. We all fear exposing the hurt places. It is so much easier to fill the holes with the same thing everyone else does—pretense, presumption, pleasure seeking, perfectionism, or mediocrity. We like fitting in more than sticking out like a sore thumb. To some extent, it is in our nature to fade into the woodwork instead of admitting we are hurt terribly. The journey of change appears too difficult and the price too high to pay.

In our comfortable places of misery, we disguise the holes in our souls, go out into the public places, mix and mingle, and attempt to live a fulfilled life. There is only one problem.

Doesn't fulfilled mean contentedly full? There is a contradiction between what we are attempting to do and what we are attempting to be! We are leaking something somewhere! Is pain leaking from the holes in our souls and sloshing all over other souls around us?

Ah, our soul—the repository of all that we think, have knowledge about, and hold in memory. It houses the often-volatile seat of our rawest emotions and is the defined place from which we choose, rightly or wrongly, the decisions that govern our behavior. That complicated inner part of us is exposed to and collides with the souls of others. We judge life from its vantage and operate according to the attitudes and platitudes stored there.

Will you join me on a journey to the core of your being, and in the simplest terms I can use, explore the profound matter of the healing of the holes in your soul? Shall we move forward toward greater wholeness? Press into better relationships and better responses in all circumstances. It really is worth it because there is nothing but gain ahead!

Oh, my, I just realized I forgot to give you the name of my doctor. His name is Jesus!

Chapter Two

Holes in Our Souls Happen Through Heredity and Environment

*H*ave you ever been compared to someone in your family album because either you looked like him or her or you did something similar to that person? "The acorn doesn't fall too far from the tree!" Ever hear that one? Perhaps you have heard, far too many times, how much like so and so you are. Maybe you have been reminded too often how much you are NOT like them. Have family members wounded your heart with arrows of negative comments?

We can draw much needed information from two sources concerning what we inherit from family and our environments. One source gives us technical information obtained through observation, testing, experimentation, and discovery. The other gives us reasons, guidelines, and wisdom for life. I am, of course, speaking of scientific knowledge from man and the book of life that comes from God—the Bible.

I believe much that science has given us is beneficial and has great worth. Medical breakthroughs, particularly in the last part of the twentieth century, have saved lives and prolonged life. Science has expanded our knowledge of the universe, far beyond what any other generation has ever known. Who can measure how the knowledge has helped affect change as deserts and once non-productive lands are reclaimed to help feed the world's masses?

But with all our advancement, we still take more lives before they begin than we save through medical advancement. War and genocide wipe out entire generations and leave orphans and widows to live in the devastation of soul and surroundings. Hatred, meanness, perversion, and jealousy do their dirty work in every place and each century of human existence. We need more than human knowledge to help us.

We inherit many things, from a crooked little toe like Momma's, to Daddy's big blue eyes. Once, only scientific testing could suggest what DNA knowledge has now confirmed. We have a blueprint imbedded in our cells. If we bear a resemblance in the visible part of our being, is it not likely we bear resemblances in the invisible part of our being as well? Is it coincidence that our over-the-top anger is just like Granddaddy Matt's or our sweet nature is just like Aunt Judy's?

When I was young, the scientific world tried to determine whether behavior was influenced more by heredity or environment. It was quite an argument. Evidence mounted steadily on both sides. Child-rearing questions piqued the interest of 1950s and 1960s society. People are interested for the same reasons today, even more so due to the serious behavioral problems we see developing in ever-younger children.

I am very grateful for, and I have benefited from scientific breakthroughs. However, I am concerned about what we do with our scientific evidence. When we take significant information and use it to project a pattern for life, it is almost like pronouncing a sentence before a life has been lived.

Scientific knowledge gives us facts to help us prepare for precarious places in life, but instills a sense that we cannot change what is in our make up. It can lead to numbing fear as well as paralyzing what-ifs. What if I get cancer like Mother? What if I have a heart condition like Papa?

A great part of life does not come from scientific observation or discovery. It originates with the mind that made all minds, the Creator and master designer of life—God Almighty. In the Bible, He talks about what we inherit ancestrally and how we deal with the environmental circumstances in which we have been raised.

8

Interestingly, the Bible accurately portrays life's truths to past generations while speaking to the present generation and projecting those truths to future generations. The Bible's knowledge and application are timeless, its truths absolute and universal.

Ancient theologians have studied it, and children barely able to read believe it. Through the ages, its timeless message has healed souls. The wealthy and the impoverished, people of every culture, on every continent, in every type of environment, have benefited from its wisdom.

Any family problem that you can imagine (or that can be made into a TV sitcom) is described in the Bible. It does not sugarcoat its stories, which include murder, prostitution, incest, robbery, injustice, jealousy, rape, and every form of abuse. The story of King David and his family includes everything just mentioned.

Even medical issues, ranging from leprosy, blindness, and childless wombs to deep depression and insanity are described in its pages. But despite anguishing sadness and great dysfunction, the stories do not all end in hopelessness. That is the good news!

From every circumstance, some individuals came to greater wholeness. No matter the dysfunction, they overcame detrimental family behaviors and their responses to difficult or even evil environments. Many went on to carry their wholeness to others. God extended an invitation to life in every age—to bring those who have been devastated by heredity or environmental influences to wholeness. Those who accepted God's invitation become testimonies of His mighty healing work. Their victories greatly encourage the hurting in every generation. Their stories speak to today's reality, although their lives ended long ago. They have been cheerleaders of God's promises for generations beyond their own and extended hope for over five thousand years.

One of my favorite stories is that of Joseph because I identify with him, especially regarding difficult family relationships. His story makes for incredible reading and can be found in *Genesis, chapters 37-45.* Countless times, I have been encouraged by Joseph's faith and God's faithfulness in restoring all that was taken from him by jealous brothers' bitter betrayal. God did an amazing healing in that broken family situation. Have I whetted your appetite to take a peek? You'll be blessed, I promise!

These are a few reasons I find the Bible a reliable source for healing the holes in my soul. Many times, I have had sound facts and expert medical advice, but my soul's needs exceeded those limits. I needed soaring hope, catapulting change, and comfort capable of piercing steel doors of pain.

On other occasions, I needed revelatory truth of emotional flaws deeply buried in myself. Still later, I craved more than facts to fill holes in my soul after the traumas of my childhood and the heart-rending experiences of young adulthood.

Before there was DNA proof, the Bible spoke about the plans God has for us. *Jeremiah 29:11 (NIV): "For I know the plans I have for you," declares the Lord, "plans to prosper you and not to harm you, plans to give you hope and a future."* How awesome to know that in sometimes-chaotic everyday life, there is a plan for my future and yours. That, too, is in our DNA!

Psalm 138:7 (NIV) speaks further to our common circumstances. *"Though I walk in the midst of trouble, you preserve my life." Verse 8* declares what God will do with my life: *"The Lord will fulfill His purpose for me; Your love, O Lord, endures forever."* We are told about trouble, but we are promised that purpose can come out of it. It depends on the One greater than all things and circumstances.

In *Psalm 121:7-8 (KJV),* God promises, *"The Lord shall preserve thee from all evil: He shall preserve thy soul. The Lord shall preserve thy going out and thy coming in from this time forth, and even for evermore."* I just love this verse. It brings comfort to my soul in life's uncertain places.

Without the promise of God's Word and evidence of fulfillment, life would be like a game of dodge ball played with a steel-plated ball against our futile defense mechanisms. That is not a winning situation! Once it is settled in our hearts and minds that there is a reliable guidebook for life written by life's architect, it behooves us to go there for sustenance and truth. This revelation jumpstarts God's healing process.

The process goes something like this: I am made aware by God through His Spirit that my truth or perception of truth is different from what God says in His book. Through exposure to God's truth, a desire begins growing (much like a small seed) to match my perception to His truth. After all, the Bible has a much longer record than I do.

In this search, examination, and application of truth, I learned some incredible things about myself, and my relationships with loved ones, acquaintances, and strangers. I found that we all share the traits of selfishness and self-protection. Both can lead to bad, destructive behaviors that affect those with whom we are connected in our world. Our behaviors reflect reactions to uncomfortable feelings like anxiety or fear that we do not want to deal with.

Humans were designed to learn by copying the actions of those closest to us. We mimic behaviors of family members as we grow up. For example, if Momma screamed at us every time we did something displeasing, chances are that we will scream at our children. Other painful feelings are stored in our hearts and imposed on others after harmful or traumatic experiences. Hurtful words can damage our soul. The soul's normally resilient fiber breaks down.

Something I have personally experienced is that irrational feelings often govern what I know to be correct behavior. I inevitably feel guilty, but I seem helpless to do anything about it. I want to do the right thing, and I know what the right thing to do is, but I choose the wrong behavior anyway.

That goes on until I am confronted with God's Word. The first thing I have to do is recognize the truth when it is shown to me. Next, I must want that truth more than I want to do what I have always done. Finally, I must ask for help from God. I have a right to His help because of what God offered to make it possible. He gave me the manual for life, He allows me direct access to Himself through His Son, and He even gives me a live-in helper—His Holy Spirit. His offer is hard to resist!

To reiterate, we receive wounds in this life from what we inherit from our family and from the environments in which we are raised. We have the opportunity to reach for help from more than one source. It is good to have the knowledge of science and to take advantage of breakthroughs in technology and medical advancement. It is even better to turn to the One who made us. We need more than knowledge. We need a healer who understands the soul. He knew what century we would be born in, the environments in which we would grow up, and the circumstances and traumas that would wound us. He also gave us the way, truth, and life in His Son to deal with the damage.

In a few chapters, I will be sharing my story about the healing of my soul. It is not yet a complete journey, but my healed wounds have changed my behavior and relationships. I no longer have the same reactions to circumstances that once overwhelmed me, and I no longer think I have the right to create my own justice.

Earlier, I asserted that God does not do His work in a solitary place. Quite the contrary is true. He has used all kinds of people to help me—counselors, ministers, teachers, family, and friends. Some have brought exposure; some have brought wisdom and insight. Still others have extended healing prayers and proclaimed me free of oppression by the devil.

Some dear ones have held me in difficult times with the loving arms of friendship. Some have simply stayed the course with me. It would take an eternity to express my gratitude to God and those He has used and continues to use in my life. I have always found it easy to give but not so easy to receive, but I have discovered I need to exercise both practices to obtain healing. Does any of this sound faintly familiar?

If so, I invite you to peek at the next chapter to see if we have other things in common. Perhaps something will cause a heart changing "yes" to come from deep inside your being. Maybe, you are not quite there, but curious. It won't hurt to read a bit further. If you have decided to accept the invitation, let's turn the page…

Holes in Our Souls Contain Toxic and Infectious Substances

In Chapter One, we went to our shared experiences and concluded that we are all holey. Our need is to go from holey to whole. We examined the two main sources from which we received those life's wounds in Chapter Two, and determined that heredity and environment contribute equally to our souls' condition. We consulted two sources about our needy souls. Although much good comes from scientific and medical understanding, the best source for healing our souls comes from God's proven, timeless Word, the Bible.

What changes occurred when the representatives of dysfunctional humanity emerged from its pages daring to disregard learned behaviors when confronted with truth? Instead of continuing harmful patterns, they were transformed. God healed their toxic, infectious soul wounds because He is the ultimate healer. Their triumphs leap forward in time to strengthen us.

I begin this chapter with one of my favorite verses on healing. I have camped out in it's truths for many years. Real joy has come with telling my story, offering hope, and watching others find healing through prayer and the truth of God's Word.

These scriptures cover both the wounding and the healing of the body, soul, and spirit. They are found in the Old and New Testament. Are you ready? Dare to begin to believe these truths. First, let's look at *Isaiah 61:1-4. (NIV)* I present it as a list of what the Lord promises to do:

The Spirit of the Sovereign Lord is on me, because the Lord has anointed me to:

1.   *Preach good news to the poor*

2.   *He has sent me to bind up the brokenhearted*

3.   *To proclaim freedom for the captives and release from darkness the prisoners*

4.   *To proclaim the year of the Lord's favor and the day of vengeance of our God*

5.   *To comfort all who mourn*

6.   *And provide for those who grieve in Zion*

7.   *To bestow on them a crown of beauty instead of ashes, the oil of gladness instead of mourning, and a garment of praise instead of a spirit of despair*

8.   *They will be called oaks of righteousness, a planting of the Lord for the display of his splendor*

9.   *They will rebuild the ancient ruins and restore the places long devastated*

10. *They will renew the ruined cities that have been devastated for generations.*

Moving on to *verses 6 and 7*, there is more (comments in parenthesis are mine):

11. *And you will be called priests of the Lord*

12. *You will be named ministers of our God*

13. *You will feed on the wealth of nations, and in their riches, you will boast*

14. *Instead of their shame, my people will receive a double portion*

15. *And instead of disgrace they will rejoice in their inheritance*

16. *And so they will inherit a double portion in their land*

17. *And everlasting joy will be theirs*

Follow as we go further in *verses 8-11:*

18. *For I, the Lord, love justice; I hate robbery and iniquity*

19. *In my faithfulness I will reward them* (Notice—it is His faithfulness!)

20. *And make an everlasting covenant with them* (Much more than a contract)

21. *Their descendants will be known among the nations, and their offspring among the peoples* (Think children and grandchildren here!)

22. *All who see them will acknowledge that they are a people the Lord has blessed* (Notice He didn't say they would understand but that they would make note of it.)

23. *I delight greatly in the Lord*

24. *My soul rejoices in my God*

25. *For He has clothed me with garments of salvation*

26. *And arrayed me in a robe of righteousness, as a bridegroom adorns his head like a priest, and as a bride adorns herself with her jewels* (What a wardrobe—and He purchases it for me.)

27. *For as the soil makes the sprout come up and a garden causes seeds to grow, so the Sovereign Lord will make righteousness and praise spring up before all nations.*

I told you it was an incredible piece of scripture. And in case you think this was just written to people in ancient Israel, go to *Luke 4:18-21.* Jesus read the scripture aloud in the temple and declared that it was fulfilled. He is the healer spoken of in those incredibly hopeful words.

Now that we have examined what it means to go from holey to whole, let's look at the toxic and infectious things we have taken out of our souls. If you will, make a list before you read mine, and see what you come up with. The following space is for your list:

1.

_____

_____

2.

_____

_____

3.

_____

_____

4.

_____

_____

5.

_____

_____

6.

_____

_____

7.

_____

_____

8.

_____

_____

9.

_____

10.

_____

11.

_____

12.

_____

13.

_____

14.

_____

15.

_____

Now, I'd like to present mine for comparison:

1. **Poverty** (feeling stolen from, deprived, less than; never getting ahead financially, always broke, envious of the "haves"; in debt, aimless, doubting the ability to get a better life; overwhelmed and hopeless)

2. **Broken-heartedness** (sense of continued loss, hurt, betrayal; sense of being in pieces, not whole; inability to trust; bitterness from which we can not seem to recover)

3. **Captivity** (physical, mental, and emotional)

4. **Imprisonment** (bad behaviors can be as confining as a prison cell)

5. **Darkness** (mental torment, addictions, habits, evil associations, occult activities)

6. **Continual mourning** (eternal sadness, overwhelming cloud on life)

7. **Unquenchable grief** (unable to come to comfort, barrenness of soul, torment of mind, inability to move on or to let go of who or what is already gone)

8. **Ashes** (speaks of destruction, failure, and ruin: nothing ever seems to succeed or have the desired end)

9. **Spirit of despair** (depression: state of inescapable doom and gloom)

10. **Ruin** (on every front—family, personal, job, social)

11. **Devastation** (on all planes of internal and external existence)

12. **Shame** (that follows as close as a shadow, even if what caused the shame ended years ago)

13. **Disgrace** (that emerges from ruin and devastation)

14. **Robbery** (of all that is precious in life)

15. **Iniquity** (a bent toward certain sins)

16. **Injustice** (done to us or by us)

Perhaps your list is longer than mine is. If you think about the fruit of some of this list's toxic substances, you can add betrayal, self-pity, self-absorption, cruelty, hatred, hopelessness, strife, divisiveness, meanness, distortion, murder, envy, and jealousy.

All of these things lead to loss of true fullness in our physical, spiritual, and mental life. The soul shrivels, and the spirit stops developing. Often the body and mind become weakened, even sickly, and the heart turns inward. A heart turned inward becomes infectious. What a way NOT to live!

The promise of *Isaiah 61* is precious because it does not just list the toxic and infectious substances of our soul, it holds out hope that these things are not meant to be in permanent residence in us. It is not our DNA imprint!

The divine Creator wants to make a great trade with us. He created us with a different list of soul ingredients than what we have been led to believe. His trade-in agreement beats any I have ever heard of! Here's the deal. I give Him the toxic substances of my soul as He reveals them to me. In return, I get new, life-bearing ones to replace them. Get ready because this is really good! Look at God's list:

1. **A special God-appointed newscaster** of good news

2. **Helping the brokenhearted** instead of being the brokenhearted

3. **Freedom** from inner bondage and torment

4. **Release** from darkness in all its forms in my mind and emotions

5. **God's favor**

6. **Comfort** for places that could never receive comfort before

7. **A crown** (girls, think "gorgeous tiara") of beauty

8. **Gladness** that is not based on plans and experiences going my way

9. **Righteousness** that is not based on my ability but on that of God's Son

10. **A garment of praise** instead of a spirit of heaviness (able to see the positive and not just the negative)

11. **Becoming a display of God's splendor** (testimonial commercials)

12. **Becoming one who remodels ruins** and devastated places (in others' lives—like those bound by dysfunction in your own families)

13. **Renewal** of heart, mind, body, and spirit (when the heart is renewed, it affects other parts of our being)

14. **Ministers to the Lord** (no pedigree required)

15. **Ministers of the Lord** (with or without a theology degree)

16. **Wealth** and riches (our life's prosperity increases)

17. **Double** what was taken from us in shame

18. **Inheritance** instead of disgrace and robbery

19. **Everlasting joy** (at the core of our being)

20. **A secure agreement** with God

21. **Clothes of salvation** (well being, righteousness, truth, faith)

Whew! What a deal! Best one I have ever seen. Best one I have ever believed in enough to try. I am still trading because of an amazing truth. When you trade with God, you never lose, never get taken, and never get used goods! You always win, always gain, and always get new and better things! My trade with God may sound simple. It is. I did not say it was easy. It does not happen all at once. Change takes sustained effort over time. It would emotionally overwhelm us to do it all at once.

The toxic substances in my life accumulated over many years through many excruciating experiences and from several different sources. Picture an onion's layers, and you have a good visual of life's process. Healing your emotional being simulates the peeling of an onion, one layer at a time.

Even though God has seen every circumstance, source, and resulting toxicity to my being, He has known from the time I was in my mother's womb that He would provide me a trade. He had other plans for my life. I highly recommend reading *Psalm 139*, which talks about God's plans, before going to bed at night. Its encouraging message is awesome. God is no respecter of persons, according to *Acts 10:34*. That means that He has wonderful plans for your life as well. Peek again at *Jeremiah 29:11*. There are no exceptions unless we choose to be an exception, and the only way that is possible is to not believe God.

You may wonder how God could provide this for everyone. He is not only God; He is the provision. He can break through impossibility because He is all-powerful. Remember the scripture reference from *Luke 4:18*, when Jesus read God's intended plan from *Isaiah 61*? He astounded those at the temple that day with the announcement that He was the fulfillment of that scripture. Possibility is a person who is also God Almighty.

According to *1 John 3:8*, Jesus came to destroy the works of the devil. A list of Satan's destructive works is mentioned in *Isaiah 61*. Jesus is the only one who can destroy the evil works because He was specially equipped and sent by His Father, Almighty God. He made Jesus able and capable. As the Son of the living God, He became the healer of all that is broken. No one else can do the job.

So how does this process start and what does it look like? First, God will give you a personal invitation through the preaching of His Word about His Son Jesus. It is because of Jesus that we receive an invitation. We listen to what the Spirit speaks through the preached Word and accept God's invitation with our hearts.

He offers us so much more than what we are asked to give Him. We get a ticket to the most spectacular, mind boggling, sought-after place of all time—heaven. We receive forgiveness for all past and present wrongdoing and promise of its extension into the future. We become immediate heirs of God's promises of freedom from addictions and life-long hurts. He offers us the wisdom of the ages from His eternal perspective. That is greater than the recorded wisdom from every culture throughout time.

This invitation involves surrender and a property exchange. The property is our life; the surrender is our control. We give Him our whole life and ask Him to give us His life in return. Our property is loaded with all the experiences and relationships that have ever been a part of our existence.

There's a whole lot of mess that He gets with our real estate! He is fully aware of that and not surprised. He has plans to take our mess, our toxic, infectious substances, including the leftover junk from poorly handled and poorly chosen relationships, and exchange them for the goods of a blessed life. Sounds intriguing, doesn't it?

This property includes the house of our life. By invitation, He will shine His light into every darkened room. If we give Him permission, He will remove the dead, devastated, ruined things and replace them with beautiful, magnificent things that will outlive us. He will fill every hole in our soul with healing life if we let Him.

In my life, He has already over-turned the torment in my mind, vindicated unjust situations with family, and exchanged my negative outlook for a positive one. He fulfilled dreams I thought were long dead and changed my sadness to joy! If you were able to see yourself without the toxicity with which you have lived, what would be different in your life?

God doesn't just give us new things for the discarded things. He teaches us how to live the new life He has for us. He provides an excellent life-coaching manual in His Word, the Bible. Don't forget His promise of a full-time, live-in soul keeper—The Holy Spirit.

Jesus will give us strength when we want to give up or give in. He will hold us as He extracts the thorns that have pricked our being. He will keep us through our screams as He carefully removes the scabs from festering wounds. He will protect us during recovery. He will change our holey life for a more whole one. He even promised that we could have a holy life. I know I like this particular trade. How about you? Want to make this trade? Is right now a good time? If so, let's pray together:

Oh, Lord, I recognize that I need to give You what I cannot change or control—my life. I am exhausted from trying. I don't understand why You would want my life with its scars, mistakes, and messes. I definitely think that You are not getting the best end of this deal.

What You offer I need so much, so please take my life and give me Yours. I understand that if I give You the sin that has resulted in the messes I have made, You, because of the price paid by your Son Jesus on the cross, will forgive me.

You will not only give me new life here on earth, but later on, I will spend eternity with You. The new life You give me includes opportunities to heal the wounds of my soul. Thank You for this incredible deal. I understand that my new life will begin immediately and last forever.

I also grasp that I am entering the process of having You transform the house of my soul through the powerful work of Your Holy Spirit, which will come to live in me. I want to take the deal You are offering me, Lord! Thank You so much for making it available to me. Amen.

Chapter Four

Holes in Our Souls Need Healing

*I*n the introduction to this book, I mentioned that the inspiration for its title came from a story about my mother who, during the Depression, daily mended the holes in the bottom of her one and only pair of shoes so she could wear them to school the next day. She camouflaged the holes by cutting out a piece of discarded cardboard and painstakingly fitting it inside the shoes. She then painted the bottom black to match the soles. How nauseating the smell of that shoe polish must have become to her.

The cardboard soles rubbed painful blisters that never had time to heal. Scabs remained soft and fresh, and the rubbing caused the blisters to pop and seep. Day in and day out, she had to rely on the same thin substitute for a real sole. Well-worn, repaired socks did nothing to ease the painful blisters, and more often than not, contributed to further pain. She walked gingerly due to her great discomfort and to avoid scraping off the shoe polish, which would give her disguise away. She could never escape her "tend to the mend" process.

My mother did not know if or when there would be a new pair of shoes for her. She did the best that she could with what she had because there was nothing better. To avoid embarrassment, she was willing to bear the pain, perform the tedious task every night, and walk as carefully as possible to avoid detection.

The materials she used were temporary. They were neither sturdy nor durable. Cardboard was never intended to be used as soles for shoes. She could not walk for long without disappointment tugging at her heels, for the holes inevitably reappeared despite her meticulous effort to hide the problem.

Isn't this a truthful, even painful, analogy of what you and I do when we have holes in our souls? We grab whatever camouflaging material is available so we can go out our front door into our world and function as normally as possible. We hope our materials last the entire day. Sometimes, however, we can only manage to cover an immediate event.

It can be disastrous if we do not tend to our soul's holes. What is inside becomes blazingly visible through our outward behavior. Those we are closest to become the recipients of whatever oozes from our unattended places. The cycle is all-consuming!

Just a small interjection. Do you find it interesting that although I have yet to mention what substances come from our wounded souls, you know what they are and have already named them in your mind?

Were any of these running through your mind—anger, fear, paranoia, meanness, spitefulness, over-bearing control, hatred, strife, divisiveness, gossip, or jealousy, just for starters? Perhaps it was dissatisfaction, negativity, doubt, or distrust. Our holes are most at home in insecurity, where many of the above-mentioned substances reside. We feel successful if we can stucco over this room as if it does not exist, but sometimes, we are blindsided. A new trauma or the memory of an ancient one arises; a dreaded someone from our past appears unexpectedly; an emotional ambush by a friend or foe comes our way. Suddenly, there is not enough time to reach for our camouflage. It is nakedly open and one or more of the obnoxious substances leaks out. What a miserable, uneasy, awful, and exposed moment! How uncomfortable for anyone within a foot of us.

If we have lived with our camouflage long enough and in close proximity to someone who loves us, we know the limitations of our cover-up techniques. Perhaps, we have grown weary of the disguise they afford. We may have even ventured out to look for help, only to find still more substitute materials.

We try them because they are new and different, but with just a few uses, we discover they are not much better than what we have been using.

So, what have you received as temporary help? Is it an ancient science, or an intellectually appealing philosophy? Is it an ordered set of positive statements to say repeatedly until they overcome the negative way you see yourself? Has a popular and particularly charismatic teacher grabbed your ear? Have you decided to try the new medication your friend's psychiatrist prescribed? Are you planning to attend that hypnosis lecture the newspaper gave such overwhelming testimonial to?

If you are a Christian, do you want an appointment with the gifted counselor the church just hired? Do you think purchasing the latest best-selling teaching CDs from the Christian bookstore will fill the void? Are you seeking a personal word from the traveling prophet coming to town next Friday? Do you believe that the leadership position on the church finance committee, with its heavy scheduled meetings and busy activities, will fill the shrouded soul hole? Has changing to a liturgical, fundamental, charismatic, or non-denominational church whetted your appetite of hope? How many things can you add to this short list to try?

As a Christian, I truly believe that some things and people just mentioned play a powerful part in the healing process, especially when we are directed to them in God's order. We need a good Christian counselor to listen patiently as we get the story of our wounding out of our secret hiding places. We need their Godly wisdom and ordered steps.

It takes excellent teachers to help us renew our minds, where old, unhealthy thought patterns once played their warped messages. There are wonderful books and tapes to take advantage of. There are gifted pastors, teachers, and evangelists who may participate effectively in the mending of our souls. Praise music is a wonderful tool as well.

Just what is the order of God? It does not necessarily occur when someone decides to point it out to us. Normally, that will not drive us toward healing. Unsolicited, it may even cause us to run the opposite direction or add it as a fresh layer to the wound itself. We may continue to blame others or circumstances rather than looking inside for what is wrong.

The first order of God does not come from others or us, but in the form of direct revelation from God's Holy Spirit, that part of God that causes us to see truth. Further, He shows us that hurt, trauma, guilt, and shame are the fruit of what God calls sin. He convicts us of our sin and points us to a savior who can deliver us from its devastating effects. The Holy Spirit reveals the truth of Jesus Christ. God's first work of soul healing is to take away the guilt and penalty of sin by giving us new life obtained by His Son's death on the cross.

This is called salvation, and it happens as we hear the truth of the Bible preached and recognize that we need Jesus, who is able to take our sin away and become righteousness for us. He causes our heart to want to accept the truth. This is not just intellectual assent. It goes much deeper, to our will, which operates the "doing" part of our entire being.

Once we have given Jesus, the Son of God, ownership of our being, accepted His forgiveness and His righteousness by the knowledge of the Holy Spirit, we are born again. This Holy Spirit, the part of God that makes it possible for Jesus to be in us, becomes our inner helper, communing with the realm of God in heaven.

The good news is that whoever is born again in Jesus is a new creation. *(2 Corinthians 5:17)* This scripture goes on to tell us that old things are passed away and all things are become new. That fact must be appropriated through active faith. The newness is absolute truth. We are as new as a freshly birthed baby, but just as a new baby must be nourished in order to grow healthy, so, too, we must receive the nourishment and truths of God's Word to grow healthy in our new life.

Unlike babies, we had our old life long before we got the new one. Therefore, as much as we must learn about new things, we must unlearn many other things. We must let truth unearth the lies woven into the experiences of our lives. This is another action of faith. It is not simply a truth I speak about and spend time studying, but one to which I yield, determined to obey God. Our built-in life coach remains to bring us revelation, healing, and wholeness. *Romans 12:2* describes this process as transformation by the renewing of our minds.

Let's take a more in-depth look at this wonderful deposit from God. The Holy Spirit has many titles and functions. He is:

1. **The Spirit of Truth,** who lives in us *(John 14:17)* and who guides us in all truth *(John 16:13)*

2. **The Indwelling Witness,** who causes us to know we belong to God, that we are in God and He is in us *(Romans 8:16, Galatians 4:6, 1 John 3:24, 1 John 4:13, 1 John 5:6)*

3. **The Teacher,** who instructs us about spiritual things *(Luke 12:12, 1 Corinthians 2:13, 1 John 2:27)*

4. **The Power of God,** who gives us the impetus and supernatural ability to live a Christian life and the empowerment to be a witness for Jesus *(Acts 1:8)*

5. **The Gift of God,** promised by our Heavenly Father to us *(Luke 11:13, Acts 2:38)*; He has gifts from God to us as well *(1 Corinthians 12:1-11)*

6. **The Fire of God,** who stirs us to service *(Matthew 3:11)*

7. **The Comforter**, who causes us to remember the works of God in our lives *(John 14: 26)*

8. **The Life Giver,** who makes our spirit alive *(John 6:63)*

9. **The One who convicts us** of sin *(John 16: 7-8)*

10. **The Counselor** *(John 16:7)*

11. **The Fruit Producer** of love, joy, peace, patience, kindness, goodness, faithfulness, gentleness, and self-control *(Galatians 5:22)*

12. **The Seal of God,** who marks us as God's for all eternity *(Ephesians 1:13)*

Because the Holy Spirit is God and lives in us following salvation, He searches our inner being with His light to find all the places that prevent us from being whole. Once the light has shined, He makes it known in our being. We are no longer in the dark. He shows us that it is in us, not outside of us. Then, through prayer, we ask for further revelation, as well as God's next ordered part of our healing. He will direct us to what we need in that next step.

It may be that He directs you to instruction in the Word through a particular teacher or pastor. He may lead you to a selected counselor. You may be drawn to a specialized ministry. Because we have all been wounded in different ways and in a different order from others, God is incredibly individualized in His process of healing. What marvelous wisdom God displays through using process! By using divinely ordered steps to heal us, He restores the very thing that has been most wounded and broken—trust. What a way to reestablish what was destroyed.

It would have been very easy for God to simply touch us. We would, I am sure, prefer that method to a systematic process, but if He were to do that, we would be deprived of the rebuilding of trust in God and others.

The rebuilding of trust comes only as we surrender to each step in the ordered process God selects for us. If we heal God's way, we get a double blessing—the healing of our soul and a restored "truster."

If you will, think back for a moment to the list of helps I mentioned earlier in the chapter. The world offers some; religion offers others. Occasionally, momentary relief comes from trying the things offered by the secular and religious worlds. However, all too often, the offerings of the secular world do not last because they rarely get to the root of infection. They medicate or sedate but do not provide permanent healing. Only the One who made us can get to that unseen, but very real place that navigates our outward functions.

I spent much of my life wanting to bury my pain by trying to help others with theirs. One day, the Lord, through His Holy Spirit, spoke to my soul, shined His light into my troubled, darkened rooms, and offered me His process of healing. I accepted and began my journey toward greater wholeness.

I suffered tremendous heart wounds as I grew from a little girl to a teenager. They continued to occur throughout my life. Now, however, my life reflects the reality of God's healing. This healing did not happen instantly. My first healing happened in my late twenties. More took place in my thirties. The greatest healing came during my forties. It is still happening as I enter my sixties.

I do not mean to imply that all I have done is look inward. This is not about the navel-gazing dungeon of introspection, although for far too many years, I visited that place several times a day. Most of the time, I felt like a gerbil running endlessly on the wheel in its cage. I circled that wheel long enough to learn that introspection is only a downward, self-absorbed spiral, not a healthy or stable stairway out of misery. Every time God healed me, He directed me to heal relationships, share in ministry, and live a blessed life that emanates from the inside out. That is the proof of true healing.

Are you conscious of an area in which you live inwardly isolated? Are there times you catch yourself spiraling downward in self-absorbed thoughts that lead you to despair rather than hope? When you look at your relationships, do you find mostly healthy ones or are you involved in some that you know are absolutely detrimental?

If you found that the answers to the questions just posed are not what you would like them to be, I would like very much to come alongside you in prayer, just as someone did for me when I began to want different answers to the same kind of questions.

Won't you ask for the healing process to begin, if you haven't already? It is my privilege to be at this place in time with you as we pray together:

Oh, Father, by Your Holy Spirit, bring revelation and an invitation to healing and fullness of trust to the wounded places of this precious soul coming to You, and please bring them confirmation in a way that this person understands that You never intended for them to remain in the pain they have suffered for so long. Please watch over them as You lead them from one place of healing to the next. We bless You for the better life that is ahead.

Thank You for the keys to overcoming the adverse situations in this dear person's life. Turn what the enemy of their soul meant for harm into the greatest good imaginable with Your power, direction, and healing.

Take away victimization, helplessness, and hopelessness. Bring understanding of what You have already provided in the course of this one's life that he or she may never have been conscious of because the pain and hurt was so great.

Please bring sense out of what once seemed senseless, meaning out of what seemed meaningless. As You mend each hole of the soul, fill them with health and wholeness. Lead this hurting heart to restoration in relationships with others. Thank You, in the mighty name of Jesus, Your Son. Amen.

Chapter Five

Holes in Our Souls Need Uncovering

I am grateful that God did not leave me the festering, wounded being He started with. He is a masterful surgeon of the heart! He knew exactly when to begin uncovering my wounds. He knew the perfect time to take off the scabs. The scabs were never intended to be permanent; they were temporary covers, to be taken off so that the wounds might be opened, the putrid infection lanced, the healing balm applied, and the recovery monitored.

My experiences contain facts and names of those who have passed on or who do not mind my sharing with you. Please do not mistake the mentioning of names with blame of any kind. These experiences have been pressed through the colander of forgiveness on both sides.

I have lived through adverse difficulties, but I am not trying to minimize anyone else's experiences. I intend nothing but to describe God's healing process in my soul, which has brought me hope and change. Many of you have survived more devastation than I can dare imagine. Perhaps something in my story will offer hope to you. May it serve to light a way out of the pit of confusion that despair and self-pity create. May you clearly see God's design for your life, which has been in place from your earliest beginnings.

God has had plans for me since I was in my mother's womb, but an enemy has also had plans in direct opposition to those of the Lord. While Almighty God had creative designs for me, the devil, the enemy of my soul, had plans of destruction. Praise the Lord, God's purpose was the winner. I pray that this truth becomes your revelation and reality, too. God is no respecter of persons. What He has done for me, He will do for you, as well!

During a wonderful Bible study a couple of years ago, the teacher requested we do a time-line of our lives. She instructed us to note on the time-line when traumatic experiences, important events, and spiritual interventions happened. It was eye opening to view my life that way. I plainly saw God's plans in the middle of a particular traumatic experience. The footprints of His victories over my enemy's plans were undeniable!

However, it was not until my soul had received some much needed healing that I was able to discern the depth of God's plan. For many years, I was too full of self-loathing and self-pity to see the truth of God's love. I had no idea He could take the trash of my life and turn it to treasure or rewrite the hopeless drama of trauma into a message of hope. He brought dark secrets to the light of truth to free my hidden identity. He exposed the torment of lies and betrayal to His love and forgiveness. He breathed His resurrected life into my shriveled soul!

Out of the good and bad, the ugly and sad, He intended to write a testimony to His glory and a new ending to my life. He even gave me new eyes that could see things from His point of view! My, what a difference that has made!

From the beginning, secrets hovered in my background—a family Bible with an inscription to my mother and me from my grandmother listed my last name as Markowitz, not Hendrix.

When I learned to read, I thought I was special to have two last names. I finally asked my mother about the mystery at age eleven. What a memorable moment that day turned out to be.

Mother told me that my dad, E. L. Hendrix, the only dad I had ever known, had adopted me after she married him. She could barely talk for the tears. In broken phrases, she told me that she and Hiemie Markowitz had divorced six months after I was born. A court case ensued, and he said some very bad things about her and tried to disown me.

I understood very little. My mother, a child of the 1930s, grew up believing that it was wrong to uncover difficult family matters. They were simply not brought out in the open. The matter that day would be given minimal coverage. Mother provided only the scantest information.

It was washday, so, following the brief discussion, she grabbed the basket of freshly washed linens and headed outside to hang them on the clothesline. She pushed the story back down into the jar of secrets inside herself and tightly screwed the lid back on. She never went there again.

My dad's mother was there that day. She also had a story to tell me. It took my mind off wishing Mother would stay in the house and help me understand. Grandmother said that the first time Mother brought me to meet her son that I ran up to him, grabbed his leg, and called him "Daddy." She said I was his from that moment on.

That story changed my focus. He cared enough to adopt me. The emphasis on his caring grew stronger when I learned that it took until I was in the second grade to pay for the adoption. I remember being very grateful for what he had done. Dad came home that night and found out that I had been told about his adopting me. He offered no further explanation but asked if I thought he had been a good enough father. I answered with an unequivocal "Yes." He then asked me not to search for my birth father. I promised him I would not. The other story of my beginning dropped into a vacant storage file in my memory.

Before the premature birth of my twin half-sisters when I was three and a half years old, I could recall Dad playing with me. He smiled and laughed a lot. But the cares of life, responsibility, and the financial load of my adoption and the hospital bills for my premature baby sisters brought out a heaviness in Dad that overshadowed the earlier playfulness I had enjoyed.

He did not often express his feelings unless he was upset or felt my sisters and I needed correcting. A heavy, underlying tension permeated our home. Dad was a good, stable man but not often demonstrative with positive vocal, physical, or emotional affirmation. After all, he had never been shown any, either.

His own father had deserted his family when Dad was just twelve. He became the responsible one in his family. He joined the navy at seventeen to serve in World War II. Following the war, he met and married my mother in 1949, taking on the responsibility of her nearly two-year-old baby daughter.

My mother had a difficult background, full of physical, mental, and sexual abuse, much of which I did not know about until I was older. As I grew up, she told me some of the stories. She was badly burned at age two when she fell into a washtub of boiling water. At eleven, she started working in a friend's restaurant washing dishes. She once saw her father drag her mother by her hair. I was too young to fully grasp that story's transparency. I just felt terribly sad for her.

Later, I understood why I felt so sad. Mother had known tremendous neglect, physical, sexual and mental abuse, and great instability. It is no wonder that she suffered throughout her life in her body and mind. Mother was physically ill a great deal of her adult life with numerous illnesses, including encephalitis, which left her with grand mal seizures. I cannot count the number of times an ambulance came to our home to take her to the hospital.

Mother's suffering escalated from the physical to the mental in her early thirties. When I was fourteen, Mother had a complete nervous breakdown and had to be institutionalized and have shock treatments. The doctors offered no hope that she would ever return home. Thankfully, the Lord had a better plan. She was home in three months.

Another problem developed that shortly overshadowed my mother's remarkable recovery. She began to drink during my sophomore high school year. Mixing alcohol with her medications for the seizures created a dangerous situation. The results traumatized our entire family. I remember going to school, terribly anxious, with a knot in my stomach and tightness in my chest. It occurred more times than I care to remember.

One day, during my senior year, I returned home to find that Mother was gone. Dad, the twins, and I had no idea where she was. Dad hired a detective, who located her in Kansas City. He also found out a great deal about her early life. Dad planned to divorce her, but decided instead to ask Mother to come home.

Mother ultimately returned home and became very active in Alcoholics Anonymous until her death six years later from an acute epileptic seizure at age forty-four. She reached out to other people throughout her remaining years. She helped many with alcoholic addictions, but still believed she had helped save me through holding on to secrets about me.

Through the years, bits and pieces of truth emerged to give me a sketchy outline of my early history. However, there remained a gnawing sense that I had never seemed to plug into my family. There were too many missing pieces, and far too many questions were unanswered. Perhaps that is why I tried to manufacture a sense of self by doing what I thought would make me acceptable to my family and others. If I were good enough at home, at church, at school, then surely my umbilical cord would finally plug into my family. As hard as I tried, my identity remained incomplete. Over the emptiness in my soul, a scab was forming hard and fast. "Doing" became the substitute for my missing identity.

That scab of misplaced identity stayed in place over my incompleteness until God, in His divine plan, chose when I was forty-three to begin its removal. That is when I learned the truth of my beginning. The revelation came shortly before the deaths of my adoptive father and one of my twin sisters. They died one month and one day apart.

God picked an incredibly painful time to begin the greatest healing of my life. The first event happened on Christmas Day 1991. Dad had trouble breathing and had to be hospitalized. His emphysema had worsened. His condition steadily improved over the next few days, and the doctors sent him home with instructions for weekly therapy. Shortly after his dismissal, I went to share some time with him and give my stepmother a breather from caretaking. That precious time turned out to be much more than I could have imagined.

Neither of us knew he would pass away less than a month later. In that special little window of time, I asked him questions about Mother and for the truth about my birth, and he began to fill in the pieces. Dad told me that Heime Markowitz was not my biological father.

Mother worked for Heime, the manager of an exclusive shoe store in Kansas City. The store belonged to an older married man with whom Mother became romantically involved. That relationship ended when she discovered she was pregnant. She started dating Heime, and they married within a relatively short time. However, due to my all-too-early arrival, the marriage ended before I turned a year old. At last, I had a significant piece of background. Although he confirmed the truth of my birth, he said no when I asked him for the name of my biological father. Even at forty-three, Dad still felt responsible for shielding me from the whole truth.

"Why?" swirled non-stop in my mind. To gain momentary peace, I simply had to accept what I could not understand. Just as Mother had, he kept what he thought was potentially harmful from me.

Dad's recovery was short-lived. He had to return to the hospital. During a routine procedure for another complication, his bowel was accidentally punctured. He passed away three weeks later, taking the remaining secret of my identity with him.

Dad had only been gone one month and one day when I received a phone call from Brenda, one of my twin half-sisters. Her news was numbing. Linda, the other twin, had just had a fatal heart attack. Could I come up to Ft. Worth to help with the funeral? I got on a plane the next morning and attended yet another family funeral.

The days following my father and sister's deaths were excruciating. One evening, I turned on the television just to put my hurting mind on cruise, and a story came on that so disturbed me I had to turn it off. A woman who lived in the projects of Kansas City had been taken into custody after she attempted to pray her mother back to life. The woman had been dead for some time.

The neighbors noticed something was wrong and contacted the authorities. Suddenly, I could not stand to listen or watch any more of the story. I did not know why, but it nauseated me. It was too close. I shuddered and changed the channel.

A few weeks after my sister's funeral, I called my mother's brother, whom I had not seen since my mother's funeral twenty years earlier. Following my mother's death, my father requested that my sisters and I not contact my mother's family because there had been a great deal of pain and mental distress caused by that side of the family. I felt released, after Dad's death, from the promise I had made not to contact my mother's relatives. The only phone number I had was my mother's brother.

I cautiously dialed the phone and within moments heard the voice of Uncle Charles, who greeted me warmly. We spent the next few minutes catching up on the past twenty years. I asked him about my grandmother and aunt. It turned out that the story I heard on the evening news was about my aunt and grandmother. I gasped at his words. It had been unbelievably painful for him. For the next moments, we shared our grief and loss together over the phone.

Although stunned by his news, I instantly connected with my uncle. I knew he had much-needed information concerning my identity. I told him I had learned the truth about Heime Markowitz from Dad shortly before he died. I added that he had not chosen to release the name of my biological father. Uncle Charles hesitated, and then finally asked, "Are you sure you want to know?"

I anxiously responded, "Yes."

Uncle Charles filled in some blank pieces of my history, and I understood why Dad had wanted to keep information from me. I came to understand something greater in the pain-filled days that lay ahead. My Heavenly Father protected me, using my adoptive father's actions, until the proper time for me to know the truth. Dad's secret was another scab God allowed to form.

In the few short months that followed, time seemed to pass in emotionless silence. The comfort I knew from the Lord in all the other losses of my life seemed to have vanished. Everywhere I looked, there seemed to be nothing but pain.

I researched the name my uncle had given me to see if I could locate my biological father. I prepared myself for the possibility that he had already passed away since he was thirty years older than my mother. At the time I began looking, he would have been in his late eighties.

In all my searching, I ended up identifying only one picture found in an old photo album of my mother's. From the description I gave my Uncle Charles, he confirmed that I had found my biological father, Samuel Culveltz. Further searching brought disappointment. I found no clues. Did I have other living siblings? The two I had shared life with died all too soon, in their forties. I struggled with the torment of a dead end and a dead family. I had to deal with tangled feelings over a picture of someone whose life I would never be part of.

The unprofitable search heightened my sense of loss and fostered a new depth of grief. I had lost my father, my sister, my grandmother, and aunt, and I felt hopelessly lost in time, space, and the agony of unanswerable questions.

Another thing happened that left me feeling even more disconnected than ever. My stepmother of eighteen years, who had been so close to my children and me, suddenly distanced herself. There had been some hurtful things said and done at the funerals of both my father and sister. What had been a trusting relationship changed overnight.

Several months after the funerals, I phoned my stepmother and relayed the hurt I had felt over things carelessly said and done. When we hung up, I thought we had worked things out. I was mistaken, for a few minutes later, my stepsister called to tell me that relationships between my family and me would end. Whatever my remaining sister heard had blocked her heart toward me as well. She also chose to cut off relationship.

My husband tried to reason with my stepmother and stepsister, but they refused to listen. I sent letters of apology and expressed my desire to work through what I had said and done. There were no replies. I could do nothing but pray and leave it in God's hands. I felt too impossibly anguished to relinquish my family at first. I agonized over every detail, and analyzed every word exchanged in that fateful phone call.

For one of a very few times in my Christian life, I thought God had abandoned me. I could not sense His presence. I screamed, "God, where are You? Haven't I had enough turmoil and loss? Where is Your comfort?"

I thought I must be an awful person. I felt dreadful, so alone and guilty for the lost relationship—not just for me, for my children. My stepmother had been a caring grandmother. I rehearsed everything I had done wrong to the point of mental and emotional exhaustion. What torment.

All relationship with the woman I introduced as my mother, not stepmother, ceased. We no longer shared holidays or family events as we had for the past eighteen years. I would never again visit the home I had grown up in since I was ten years old. My only remaining sister refused to be part of my life. I could not make sense of or find God's purpose in the situation at all.

It was the most incredible pain I had ever known. The hurts piled one on top of another with such dizzying speed I could not catch my breath. It was as if I was naked in the Sahara Desert, my mouth full of sand. I could see no relief in sight. I recently found a scripture that uses a similar description. *Jeremiah 17:6 (KJV): "For he shall be like a shrub of a person naked and destitute in the desert; and he shall not see any good come, but shall dwell in the parched places in the wilderness in an uninhabited salt land."*

At the time, I did not understand that God would use these circumstances to free me from the bondage of unworthiness, the bottomless pit of emotional pain, and the prison of not knowing my identity. These events in hindsight brought much needed insight!

In not truly knowing who I was, I began helping others who were hurt or victimized. I became a Christian at age eleven and considered it the only thing good or acceptable about me. Being a Christian became my entire identity for the next thirty-two years.

One afternoon, following the heart-numbing losses, I called a dear friend that I worked with in lay ministry to tell her that I had begun to shake and could not seem to stop. She immediately came over to talk and pray with me. As we prayed, she said, "I am hearing the word 'identity' from the Lord."

When she spoke that word, I felt as if a knife were cutting into my soul and shook even more violently.

"Sharon, what would there be to love about you if you were not a Christian?" she asked.

Without hesitation, I replied, "Absolutely nothing!"

Her next statement gripped my soul. "Sharon, that is a lie from the pit of hell!"

I had ministered to so many others about God's love, but now it pierced the seat of my own heart. For the first time, I recognized that particular truth was for me.

God owned that moment. It was time for my soul to emerge from captivity. She continued to pray for the Lord to break the bondage of lies I had believed all my life. I stopped shaking. Truth unlocked my prison. With that prayer, another step in the process of freedom began.

Why the Lord chose the timing He did, I do not know. I have asked why it took so long to come to my heart. When I look back, I understand that had any of the circumstances leading up to that moment happened in any other order or one moment sooner, my mind might have let go just as my mother's, my grandmother's, and my aunt's had done. The devil's agenda calculated my mental breakdown, but the Lord had the opposite plan. God desired me to have a sound mind, a liberated soul, and healed emotions in His perfect timing.

My friend's prayer that afternoon started healing my wounded soul. God destroyed the lie that the real me was unlovable and unwanted. I began to dare to get to know the Sharon I had put away so long ago—the one I thought no one wanted. I let the truth drop from my head into my heart. It was as if I had been swinging on a trapeze all my life over a pit of oozing pain, often falling in.

Occasionally, I would climb out and get back onto the trapeze, only to fall off into that hideous hole again.

Now God sent another trapeze my way. I could not reach for it until I let go of the one from which I had been swinging. With sweaty palms, a nervous stomach, and a grain of faith, I reached out, grabbed hold of the new trapeze as it swung by, and flew out over green pastures and still streams. Overhead, beautifully blue skies and comforting light calmed my anxieties.

God's trapeze was His truth. He had fearfully and wonderfully made me. He claimed me as His daughter. I belonged to royalty. I read what He said about me in the Bible. I loved what I read in *Psalm 139*. He told me He had known me in my mother's womb. His thoughts of me were so numerous they could not be counted.

I let go of the lie that I was worthless, that I did not belong, that I was pitiful, that I was ugly, that I was unwanted. The process of transformation began when I started believing God and forgave those who had caused me pain. My Christian persona had forgiven, but the shut-away Sharon had not.

The scab came off; forty-three years of infectious hurt came out. He lanced the boil of blame that I had masked through helping others. I could forgive with my head and the seat of my being—my heart. How awesomely freeing!

But there would be more than soul healing. Restoration lay ahead. God did not just empty me; He began to put my life back together. He showed me how great His work had been. Seven years after the separation, a remarkable reunion with my stepfamily began. During the estrangement, my stepsister became a Christian. She wrote a letter and asked me to forgive her. The opportunity to give and receive forgiveness with my stepsister and stepmother opened to me.

Restoration with my half-sister, Brenda, eventually came as well. When our sister Linda died, I drew a charcoal portrait of the three of us as children for Brenda. I tried unsuccessfully to give it to her on two separate occasions.

When Linda died, she didn't leave a will. Brenda took almost six years to tie up the loose ends of Linda's estate. By law, the state entered into the settling of the estate, and assessed and divided Linda's remaining property. I received a small check in the mail with a letter from Brenda's attorney.

Shortly after, Brenda asked if I would consider giving her the money from the check the state sent. I wrote that I would if she would meet with me. She chose to drive to my home, some three hours from hers, and allowed me to hug her. She also accepted the portrait I had done for her. I gave her the check, we talked briefly, and she left.

Due to the work God had done in me, I received God's restoration with my sister. She came as close as she could. Three months later, she passed away of a massive heart attack. It was another extremely difficult time, but because God had uncovered other wounds and begun healing them, the circumstances surrounding her death left me with comfort and sustained peace. No more buried fear of loss and abandonment. I could experience loss without fear because it had been exposed to God's healing touch.

I pray that as you read this chapter, you will want the Lord to do what He did to begin my healing—take away the scabs and uncover the wounds. He awaits your invitation so that He can begin His restorative work. Be comforted, dear hearts, divine healing is on the way. If the Holy Spirit has shed light on any place inside you that may need to be uncovered, will you pray the following with me?

Father God, as I read this chapter, Your Spirit began to reveal to me that I have scabs inside that You must remove. I ask for Your revelation and the blessed security of Your presence. You are aware of my fear to 'go there' and the hesitation I feel to trust You.

Please know that despite my present fear, I am reaching out to Your incredible promise. With shaky feet and trembling heart, I head in faith's direction. Where my 'truster' has been damaged, mend it. I do not want to remain where I have been. I do not want to be known for my wounds but for Your glory.

As simply as I know how, I reach out to You and trust that You will not harm me even as You uncover my wounds. Thank You, Jesus, for what You are about to do for my great good and Your undeniable glory. Amen

Chapter Six

Holes in Our Souls Need Lancing

*I*t is time to talk about one of the more difficult parts of the healing process: the lancing of the soul's wounds. I decided to draw on an analogy with which many of us who are mothers are familiar. It requires us to go to the deepest places in the reservoir of motherly love. It takes us where we do not want to go and would never volunteer to be.

Do you remember your crying child running in the back door from play, holding his arm, blood dripping on your freshly mopped tile, looking to you for help? You immediately washed the blood off the wound, carefully poured hydrogen peroxide over it, applied some A&D ointment, and bandaged it with gauze and a few Mickey Mouse band-aids. Then you kissed the wound, dried his tears, and sent him back out to play.

A few days later, you notice something is wrong. The wound has not healed. It is extremely red and the redness is going up the arm. There is yellow puss oozing from the sides of the soft scab. The infection is undeniable. Instantly, your observation triggers new thoughts about what must be done. Primal understanding kicks in immediately. A deeper level of mothering must now take over. You know your love will require actions beyond what your child will be able to grasp. All that the child knows is that his pain is at its absolute limit. He is oblivious to the danger that can result if the poison is not extracted from the body immediately. Your child cannot tolerate the thought of further pain, but you can.

As a mother, you are not only willing to go beyond the present and very real pain your child is experiencing, you are determined to go past your child's mounting screams of "No, no way," the accusations of "You don't love me," or even worse, the scathing, intimidating "I hate you!"

You will do all the comforting possible, which includes explaining the upcoming process in soothing tones, drying tears with the nearest clean cloth while holding back your own, and promising that it will be much better very soon.

Next, you put that child where he is secure. If necessary, you have someone restrain your child. For this particular wound, no topical anesthetic will affect a cure.

This fact sinks into your heart, where conflicting emotions rage, as intense as the pain your child is suffering, but you cannot possibly let that show. You must offer no face other than one that is supremely confident and reassuring.

In these moments, you grab the hem of God's grace. Perhaps you revisit the storehouse of memories of personal healing experiences. Whatever you decide, you remain resolute. Your child is incapable of doing this for himself. The toxic substance in the festering wound will poison his whole body if not lanced. You reach for the vehicle of faith where, indeed, God will give you strength and sufficient grace for what you are about to do. Courage rises.

Finally, you are ready to lance the festering, painful wound. With a prayer on your lips, having prepared as much as possible, you take the chosen instrument in hand. Despite your expertise, your heart beats fast. You steady your hand, and with tenacious determination lower it to the wound. There it is—the all-important cut. The harmful infection is coming out. You breathe a deep sigh, though your child's cries are still ringing in your ears. You finish cleaning up the remains of infection before applying medicine and giving instructions for how to care for the wound.

It is important for the child to keep the wound clean, to apply medicine at the appointed time, and to avoid anything that could puncture the healing wound and re-infect it all over again. You will remind him and check on him until the wound heals to nothing more than a faded scar.

I hope you stayed with me through my rather grueling description. Perhaps my analogy broke down somewhere around the lancing description. If you are like me, you would not be able to bear this process with your own child without great support. There were times I could hardly get through a bad diaper, much less a severely infected wound.

That is why I am so blessed that the One who lances our souls' wounds performs surgeries like this without wincing. His eyes are set on our complete healing. He will never leave us while He lances our wounds. He works with a steady hand. He douses us with His supreme grace, sufficient perseverance, and perfect patience. He will see us through the entire painful experience. He even brings in special assistants to help us through the delicate procedure.

I used the analogy of a lanced wound to depict a very spiritual process. God operates outside time and space from the place where He knows all things and can do all things—the supernatural realm. He has seen our life from every angle and every moment we have lived. Nothing has escaped His view. He knows every hurt and trauma. He also knows the work that the devil has done to bind our lives with mental, physical, and spiritual bondage. He, too, exists in that supernatural realm.

The devil does not work alone. He sends out his demonic helpers like terrorists to inflict as much damage as possible on the lives of those of us who suffer. They are on assignment to keep us bound as tightly as necessary to prevent escape. But God unbinds us and takes down the strongholds that the enemy and his henchmen have set up in the unseen realm. The Almighty deploys His angelic forces on our behalf. They are stronger than the enemy's are. God also uses human beings in the natural realm to help free us from Satan's vicious power.

He uses those who are trained and licensed in medicine, psychology, and counseling. He uses those whom He has trained in spiritual matters. These individuals have unique skills and insight. One group often works as a team in a ministry known as deliverance. Put in the simplest terms, deliverance is freedom from the bondage of the enemy. God's servants assist through special power-filled prayers for freedom. God has given them spiritual gifts, which are spoken of in *1 Corinthians 12: 4-7.*

For example, in praying for deliverance of the soul, God may use one who has the supernatural gift of knowledge to diagnose what needs to be lanced. He may direct another person on the ministry team to employ His gift to distinguish between spirits working in the spiritual realm to bind the one seeking freedom. God will give that person what spiritually needs to be prayed against in order to bring freedom. God's power, released through prayers of His ministry team, will break the enemy's hold. Once that has taken place, and the infection is extracted, God guards the freed soul from re-infection with instructions from His Word and reminders from the Holy Spirit.

He pricks our hearts when we are in situations that could open us to re-infection or even fresh wounding. God leaves no aspect of our keeping to chance. No minute detail escapes His all-seeing eyes and compassionate heart. Because He is our maker, He personalizes our healing process. We will all experience His lancing if we submit to it. How He performs the procedure and what instrument He chooses to use may vary. He knows the moment our wound must be lanced. There is no guessing! His supreme, perfect knowledge is at work.

He made us, and therefore, He knows how we are put together. He knows who and what to use as our personal lancing instruments. He begins with a counselor or a book—maybe a particular program or sermon. Perhaps He chooses a series of lessons from a gifted teacher, or even a wise mentor. For still another individual, God uses a painful family situation to expose the need for soul surgery.

When our soul wound becomes fearfully apparent, God doesn't coerce us to come to Him for the lancing of our wound. He does not restrain us if we choose to run away. He waits patiently for us, even when we choose to try other means to heal our infection. Limited and sometimes unwise human decisions often bring us to a place of great desperation. Infection spreads rapidly throughout our being until we hardly have the strength to cry for His help. Yet, no matter how faint our voice, His ear hears. Just as a shepherd can distinguish the cries of individual sheep, so the Lord God can hear our singular cry.

He not only hears us, but He responds with what is necessary. He has the instruments chosen, ready to perform emergency surgery, before we ever send out that barely audible plea for help. He directs us where and to whom we need to go from the beginning of the process to the end.

I cannot reiterate how completely Jesus knows our being, understands our wounding, and wants to lance those infected wounds that harm us. He earned the right to be the one to lance and heal our wounds. He willingly subjected Himself to man's worst wounds and infection. Not once does scripture record that He was surprised, appalled, or incapable of handling what He saw or experienced. Although He dealt with each person that came to Him with compassion, He fearlessly lanced that person's soul wounds when asked.

Soul healing begins with lancing. We cannot bypass this step. Although lancing a wound is more painful than the wound itself, fortunately, that pain lasts for a shorter amount of time. Lancing opens the exit for infection, creating a place that needs to be filled with healing medicine.

I encourage you to take a courageous step—perhaps the bravest one you have ever attempted. Will you ask Jesus to lance your wounds, if you have not already done so? He longs to hear a prayer that gives Him permission, so that the cleansing of your soul's wounds can begin. The operating room of God's heart and the healing hands of His Son are ready to receive you! Are you ready to get on the gurney? Angels are in attendance, dear one.

Chapter Seven

Holes in Our Souls Need Filling

O nce the holes in our souls have been lanced and cleaned, it is time for them to be filled in. It has never been in God's design for us to have a gaping hole. He promises in *Jeremiah 30:17, "For I will restore you to health, and heal your wounds, declares the Lord." (NIV)* The maker of Heaven and Earth, the Creator of all mankind, does not partially heal our wounds.

So what kind of medicine can fill a wound and cause it to shrink until there is only a faint scar? Where does it come from? I have wonderful news! It comes from the same source that made us. God devised its chemistry. It contains elements obtained by the death, burial, and resurrection of Jesus Christ. In fact, the chief medicinal application is what the blood of Jesus did for us when He died on the cross. This balm is timeless, effective, available to all who ask for it, and it lasts forever! How can this be?

Because Jesus died for the main cause of wounds—sin, none of its destructive forms, devastating effects, or nauseating habits are beyond the healing effectiveness of His blood. He lived as one of us and walked among us. He was exposed to the brunt of every kind of wound—body, soul, and spirit. Man lied to Him and about Him. Followers betrayed Him. Superficial hearts flattered Him with temporary accolades. His Jewish brothers praised Him as their long awaited Messiah one day and cursed Him as the embodiment of the worst evil the next day. His enemies misrepresented, maligned, spit on, maliciously gossiped about, and taunted Him. The most prestigious religious leaders questioned His authority and openly cheered His crucifixion. The ones whose hands He had fashioned beat Him until He was unrecognizable. His most faithful disciples, with whom He had shared the mysteries of heaven and taught God's secrets, abandoned Him at His most critical hour of need.

And if that were not enough, ignorant, imperfect humanity crucified Him because He lived the one and only perfect human life. They did not bruise Him for bad behavior but for the best behavior ever displayed. He never lied, cursed, killed, harmed, abused, hurt, lusted, gossiped, or treated anyone unjustly. He never once hated, not even His worst enemy.

He always blessed, served, and gave to others rather than took from them. He loved everyone He ever met—even His most ardent betrayers, who cursed Him. He was always kind, even when He found it necessary to rebuke or correct. His demeanor was firm, not controlling. He was not just truthful; He was Truth. He had a gracious manner and a heart brimming with mercy. He was the author of life who willingly lay that down to die one of the most excruciating deaths devised by humanity—crucifixion.

His works were marvelous and miraculous. He conquered evil at every turn yet submitted to its effects. He did so to obtain for us the most powerful medicine in all of history, in all of eternity. He is worth going to, not only for the stuff He has to give, but also for the stuff of which He is made.

I went to Him for the stuff my holey soul needed. I shared a few experiences in Chapter 5. Now, I want to include a bit more of my story, in the hopes that it will encourage you to examine the marvelous and miraculous works of Jesus for yourselves.

To say that, as a child, I was filled with insecurities, would be a gross understatement. I looked everywhere for someone to be. I did not care much for the little skinny waif with enormous scarred knees, no eyebrows, and all-too short bangs whose image stared back at me in the mirror.

My search for significance began early. In the first grade, I was the shortest girl in my class next to Janine Cox. She and I stood next to one another in school pictures. I also had the shortest bangs. Mother always thought my bangs needed to be cut before any major event—like school pictures.

By the third grade, I thought I had found the perfect someone to be like. She was the most beautiful, blond-headed, blue-eyed girl in my class. Her big, almond-shaped eyes looked out from underneath incredibly long, dark eyelashes. As if they were not enough to demand everyone's attention, she was blessed with the most gorgeous dimples and amazing smile I had ever seen.

I knew I could never manufacture the dimples, but somehow, in my misguided nine-year-old zeal, I thought I could make my eyes look like hers if I simply opened them wide enough. Never mind that my eyes were green or my eyelashes much shorter and too light to see!

Time rolled around for school pictures. I was on the front row, ready to try my experiment as soon as the photographer said smile. I waited in great anticipation for the finished pictures to be delivered. But when the day finally arrived and my teacher, Mrs. Hall, passed them out, I realized immediately that I had failed miserably. I looked like an advertisement for a Freddy Krueger movie! My eyes were big all right—and totally surrounded by white.

Discouragement did not overtake me. It would be a long time before I could use makeup, and I could not change my face, but there had to be something I could try. I needed some kind of gimmick that could make me special. There were plenty of beauties to look at. Hollywood movies offered so many choices! Susan Hayward had a walk that was, in my opinion, to die for.

I practiced at home in my room until I felt ready to try it out at school. I found a gimmick all right, but unfortunately, it made me notorious, not special. My insecurities fell all over themselves with each gliding stride I attempted. My walk resembled the waddle of a lame duck more than the graceful glide of Susan Hayward. I did not draw the glowing admiration of my classmates, only their soul-maiming laughter.

I decided that since I enjoyed school, perhaps making good grades was a possibility. I did not brim with natural genius, so I needed to put in many study hours. It seemed that this particular endeavor had promise. My report cards began to have more and more A's. I grew harder and harder on myself. Being a good student became a significant piece of my fragile, synthetic identity.

With time, I added being a good daughter, a good friend, a good "whatever" to the repertoire of my identity. It never seemed to improve a single thing I felt about myself. Being good outside helped cover tormenting "pictures" inside my head. They were far too gross to tell anyone about.

I began having bad dreams before age six. They always concerned "private parts." At age six, I did not understand the images in my mind. When I saw people, I saw "private parts." As a teenager, I would hit my head against the wall in an attempt to make the images go away. I kept the shameful secret of the hellishness inside and continued to be "good" outside. I could not bear the thought of anyone knowing the awful inside me.

When I became a Christian at age eleven, I felt new and clean, and the terrible images briefly went away. Then, to my horror, they returned, even during sermons at church. I prayed and tried harder to be good, still telling no one about the torment that flashed uninvited on the big screen of my imagination.

In high school, I dated mostly friends. I kept my moral standards rigidly high. I filled my time with part-time work, studies, and church activities. Inside my home, my mother went through her physical and mental crises. More and more, she slipped from reality. I never knew what might happen to her next. My sisters and I took on more household responsibilities. During this time, the images in my head went away. I will come back to this in a later chapter.

God ultimately blessed my consistent study habits. I had the honor of being selected salutatorian of my graduating class in 1965. Since I could not afford college away from home, I chose a local college where, in the spring of 1966 I met and fell in love with a young man who, like myself, had mistakenly signed up for two classes at the same time and had to drop one. We ended up in the same class.

Jim Milliman and I had more in common than that late afternoon English class. I find it interesting that when we have deep wounds, we are often drawn to someone who also has deep wounds and similar life experiences. Hints of impending struggle infiltrated our relationship from the beginning. One week, Jim thought he wanted to date only me. The next week he was unsure. Blinded by my love, I thought the uncertainty on his part would eventually stabilize.

We were young in the very destabilizing days of the draft, Vietnam, and the assassinations of Martin Luther King and Robert F. Kennedy. Jim received his "Uncle Sam Wants You" letter at the end of the summer of our freshman year in college. That letter marked a stabilizing point in our relationship. He asked me to marry him after he returned from the army. I agreed and waited for three more years.

We married thirteen days after he returned from his yearlong tour of duty in Vietnam. We divorced thirteen years later. Our dating struggles had only been on hold. They returned within the first two weeks we were married. I thought my love and commitment would be enough to overcome the struggles. I was not new to struggle, adversity, or waiting, and I was still young enough to believe that everything could be fixed with a combination of faith, effort, and commitment, even if it were only on my part. Unfortunately, it took me a long time to realize I could never fill in the holes in Jim's life. If success had merely depended on trying to help, perhaps our marriage would have not made the casualty list. The only badge I ever won was a martyr's. What a sad and lonely prize it turned out to be. Blinded by the holes in Jim's life, my own holes grew deeper from neglect.

It takes more than being privy to miracles to save a holey marriage. I hadn't had children after ten years of marriage. One Wednesday night at church, our pastor prayed for all the barren women. Twelve of us came up to be prayed for, and a year later, all twelve of us brought our "miracles" to the baby dedication service. James Joseph was bundled up in the cutest little yellow outfit for his debut. Nineteen months later, miracle number two arrived—David Jeremy Milliman.

What precious gifts the boys were to Jim and me, but even our miracles were not enough to fill in the places that grew wider between my husband and me. I could no longer "fix" the problems of infidelity and alcohol that plagued my marriage, or teach high school full time and mother two children nineteen months apart. My martyrdom finally halted; I had to turn in my badge. My "tryer" wore out, and my marriage ended.

Great neediness rose up in me as a woman, a person, a Christian, and a mother. I had come to the end of my ability, my reason, and for a moment, what I understood of my life of faith. My prayers became, "Please, help me, Lord, because I can no longer help anyone, including myself."

I no longer identified myself as the "super Christian with all the answers." I had become a minefield of battle-scarred holes. No longer could I counsel anyone else about anything. I was the one in need.

From the first words of my prayer, the Lord began to implement His plan. The gaping places were scattered throughout my being. Some were in my mind, some in my emotions; many were in my heart. I needed the powerful, transforming work of Almighty God to touch my aching heart, unstable emotions, and exhausted mind. With His healing touch, I began at age thirty-four to walk out a set of healing steps. At the time, I thought I was getting all there was of healing. Patiently and lovingly, the Lord ordered those first steps, all the while knowing that the greater part of my healing was still nine years away!

The road ahead included journeys back to points of original wounds. I came across Forgiveness Avenue and Forgiving Place. Suddenly, new road signs emerged: Deliverance Junction, Renewal Overpass, Restoration Highway, Leave-the-Past Gap, and Look Ahead Lookout, just to name a few. Certain familiar scriptures I read as if for the first time. I no longer read them to minister to someone else, but as life-giving substance for my life. Although I knew Jesus as my loving Savior, I found Him now as the One who understood my scarred places of suffering. Read this portion of *Isaiah 53 with me* from the *New Living Translation:*

> *[Jesus] was despised and rejected—*
> *a man of sorrows, acquainted with deepest grief.*
> *We turned our backs on Him and looked the other way.*
> *He was despised, and we did not care.*
> *Yet it was our weaknesses He carried;*
> *it was our sorrows that weighed Him down.*
> *And we thought His troubles were a punishment from God,*
> *a punishment for His own sins!*
> *But He was pierced for our rebellion,*
> *crushed for our sin.*
> *He was beaten so we could be whole.*
> *He was whipped so we could be healed.*
> *All of us, like sheep, have strayed away.*
> *We have left God's paths to follow our own.*

Yet the LORD laid on Him
the sins of us all.
He was oppressed and treated harshly,
yet He never said a word.
He was led like a lamb to the slaughter.
And as a sheep is silent before the shearers,
He did not open his mouth.
Unjustly condemned,
He was led away.
No one cared that He died without descendants,
that His life was cut short in midstream.
But He was struck down
for the rebellion of my people.
He had done no wrong
and had never deceived anyone,
But He was buried like a criminal;
He was put in a rich man's grave.
But it was the LORD's good plan to crush Him
and cause Him grief.
Yet when His life is made an offering for sin,
He will have many descendants.

I am so very grateful that I dared to begin believing these scriptures and accepting the truth that I was one of His heirs. He knew my suffering because He experienced more than can be imagined for all of us, not just me. As His heir, I also learned why He was called and chose to suffer. He suffered for more than mere understanding; He suffered to "fix" our brokenness. He desired that we be living testimonies of the truth of His healing.

Listen once more to verses from *Isaiah 61* from the *New Living Translation*:

The Spirit of the Sovereign LORD is upon me,
for the LORD has anointed me
to bring good news to the poor.

He has sent me to comfort the brokenhearted
and to proclaim that captives will be released
and prisoners will be freed.
He has sent me to tell those who mourn
that the time of the LORD's favor has come,
and with it, the day of God's anger against their enemies.
To all who mourn in Israel,
He will give a crown of beauty for ashes,
a joyous blessing instead of mourning,
festive praise instead of despair.
In their righteousness, they will be like great oaks
that the LORD has planted for His own glory.
They will rebuild the ancient ruins,
repairing cities destroyed long ago.
They will revive them,
though they have been deserted for many generations.
Foreigners will be your servants.
They will feed your flocks
and plow your fields
and tend your vineyards.
You will be called priests of the LORD,
ministers of our God.
You will feed on the treasures of the nations
and boast in their riches.
Instead of shame and dishonor,
you will enjoy a double share of honor.

God intended His Son to leave the awesome wonders of heaven and live on earth. He chose to subject Him to every broken place in humanity and expose His divine treasure to the ever-volatile, often unpredictable human nature. He had healing from the inside out for mankind on His omnipotent mind!

God sent His Son to earth as a man to personally experience wounding. He was blamed, unfairly imprisoned, unjustly accused, and exposed to vile evil because He understood His Father's requirement to purchase back wholeness for humanity.

He made us, and He wanted us to have complete restoration even from evils of our own choosing.

In all that we have examined about Jesus together, isn't it amazing that no matter what man or the devil subjected Him to, He remained full of things so opposite to what filled us following life's wounding? Doesn't it make you wonder what filled Him? We already know the good news; He wants to give us what filled Him!

Jesus embodied love in the face of maniacal hatred. He had joy in the midst of constant misunderstanding, faithfulness in the presence of his own disciples' heart-rending betrayal. He pressed through with strength of purpose in the pain-filled brokenness of physical beatings and patience in the clamor of false accusation. He exuded peace in turbulent storms, goodness before diabolical evil, and self-control in crowds who lost control. He remained meek in the jaws of murderous religious pride. He was gentle in the presence of wrist-binding, whip-lashing conquerors.

Ultimately, this awesome God-man brought every ounce of His suffering to a Roman cross. There, by His choice of will, working from the love and forgiveness in His soul, He died for all of us. Three days later, Jesus came back from the dead, bringing the keys of death, hell, and the grave with Him.

Is there any wonder Christians talk about the blood of Jesus with shouts of victorious praise? Doctors tell us that life is in the blood. Eternal life and life worth living is in the blood of Jesus that flowed out of Him over two thousand years ago. He lived in humanity's flesh in a sinless state. He died in a broken, beaten, crucified body for the sin of every person who has ever lived. He broke sin's binding penalty. He purchased freedom for every man, woman, boy, and girl from Satan's torment of body, mind, and emotions. He recalled the gall of injustice, the binding iniquity of generational sin, and the imposing sentence of eternal hell.

Three days after dying for mankind, He rose from the grave in the power of resurrection. His body was recognizable, but very different from the one He lay down on purpose three days before. He displayed one more heirloom purchased with His death. It is also a preview of the resurrection to come for all of us—a spiritual body that can go from this earth to God's dimension. It is glorious in appearance and whole in every sense.

I hope that you are anticipating getting to the One who is the medicine your soul needs. I encourage your heart to receive these truths. Do not fear letting Jesus fill your soul with the greatest medicine of all time—Himself! What do you think about this prescription from God? The information page on this prescription says that there are no side effects. The ingredient list includes peace of mind, greater wholeness of being, and unbelievable blessing! You can renew your prescription as needed. Turn it in at the available counter of prayer.

Father God orchestrated the entire procedure. His Son, the Divine Physician, wrote the dosage directions. The pharmacist, the Holy Spirit, will administer any change in dosage or number of times to use the medicine. He may also direct you to appointed earthly helpers such as counselors, ministers, and doctors as needed.

Written instructions are included with the prescription, direct words from the Divine Physician, pivotal in the healing process. The Bible serves as a source of instruction and transformation. Its scriptures offer confirmation of the patient's progress.

Some expected results include release from torment, addictions, and generational sins; absolving of guilt and shame; and inner joy and sense of well-being. The patient can expect improvement in himself and in his or her relationships.

I am delighted to give you my testimonial regarding the effectiveness of this prescription and the accompanying instruction book. They have worked for many years and continue to be as curative and transformational as the first time I made up my mind to try them.

Chapter Eight

Holes in Our Souls Need Forgiveness, Forgiving, and Time

Nine times out of ten, the holes in our souls have been caused by events or trauma. Both involve people: we, as victims and they, as perpetrators. Perhaps in other times, we have been the perpetrators and they have been the victims. It should not surprise us that our soul's healing requires time, forgiving, and forgiveness.

Forgiveness and forgiving: I have purposely used both the noun and the verb form. When we need to do it, forgiveness takes on the verb form; when we need to receive it, forgiveness becomes a noun. Both require faith. Both are a process. Both take two persons—God and us. Does it surprise you that I did not say it needs the presence of the person who caused the event or trauma? That is because God commands us to forgive if we want to be forgiven. *(Matthew 6:14-15)* We must deal with our heart's stuff, and we must deal with God's. Guess who has the biggest heart.

Do you know why it works this way? If we don't forgive, the past trauma and the perpetrator remain on our mind's computer screen in the here and now, as much as it did at the time it happened. It eats at peace like a cancer. It continues to grow unless we obey God and eradicate it. Our ability to forgive comes from the greatest act of forgiveness, which occurred for all of mankind, present company included.

God's act of forgiveness occurred on a rustic cross on a hilltop in Jerusalem two thousand years ago. God forgave every hideous evil, binding sin, and generational iniquity. The blood His Son shed renews the hope of mercy every day. To benefit from this act, we must go to the source of forgiveness, receive

Him as a gift, and then we will have the power and authority to forgive as we are commanded by Almighty God, our Heavenly Father.

And the result? True freedom from the torment of memories and pain bleeding into our present world and thoughts. Our hearts are carriers of bitter impurities without the touch of His heart. He loves to forgive us. He knows we need forgiveness to live and freedom from the guilt and shame of what we have done—or what has been done to us. He is aware of our need to forgive so that no flypaper hangs in our hearts and mind for the unkind deeds of others to stick to.

We need to run through the hallway of forgiveness while on our way to forgiving, but first, it must be installed in the house of our inner being by our acknowledgement that we are sinners to the core. We call on the name of Jesus, the eradicator of sin and ask Him to forgive us and take complete ownership of our lives. That is the basis for us to be forgiven and to be able to forgive others. Without confronting our own sinfulness head on, seeing our great need and helplessness without forgiveness, we cannot truly grasp the need to forgive anyone else.

Once the hallway of forgiveness has been installed, we are required to keep it clear of resentment brought on by new offenses. Because there is no sin that God will not forgive me for, there is no sin for which I cannot forgive others. When I forgive, I do not assign guilt or innocence, nor do I pass sentence or seek revenge. I rid my hallway of bitterness and rancor. God reigns as the supreme just judge. Just because I choose to forgive great injustice done to me does not mean that the offense goes unpunished. The author of absolute justice passes sentence and assigns punishment for evil deeds.

Some years ago, the Lord gave me a tool to use when going through forgiveness that I need to do or that I am helping someone else to do. He showed me a wheelbarrow. I asked, "Why a wheelbarrow?" (The Lord knows that it would not be on my normal list of feminine must haves!) He showed me that it couldn't be used correctly without picking it up with both hands.

Next, I saw the person I needed to forgive. I took a piece of paper and a pen and made a list of every offense for which I needed to forgive this person. I attached the list to that person, placed him in the wheelbarrow, picked up both handles, and rolled it over to Jesus. Next to Him stood the cross, with a curtain of His blood coming from it. That cross took all my sin and the same blood covered my guilt and shame.

The next step involved prayer. Standing before Jesus, I said, "Lord, I am here with —— and my list of offenses. Because I want You to always forgive me, I choose, by an act of my will in obedience to Your command, to forgive the person for—" And I rattled off the list of offences. I also added, "Lord, You know I don't feel like doing this. You never said I had to feel like it. You only said that I was to do it. I thank You that because I have done this, You will change my feelings."

Next, I faced that person. That was significant, especially if I was forgiving someone who had passed away. I spoke my forgiveness to the Lord as well as that person. Once I had done that, I rolled the wheelbarrow, that person, and the list to the cross and into the curtain of His blood. As I released the handles, I prayed, "Jesus, help me to see this soul, not through my eyes of his or her offense, but through your eyes." It always amazed me how my view changed and remembrance of my own forgiven sins washed over me. Hatred and bitterness crumble in the presence of an ever-forgiving God.

Forgiveness comes from a very deep work. In no way am I attempting to trivialize the process with the simplicity of this tool. It has been very powerful in the "how to" part of forgiveness through the years. Sometimes, the hardest person to forgive has been myself, but once I realized that to not forgive myself was to pompously declare that the blood of Jesus was ineffective, that I was putting myself above God—oops! Definitely a wrong mindset! Definitely a wrong position to be in! No offense retains the right to remain in my hallway of forgiveness—not even my own!

Because the events and traumas of our lives happened over years, a third requirement is needed in God's plan for our lives—time. I remember a prayer in which I specifically asked the Lord why healing took so long? I remember even more vividly the answer He gave me. It came in the form of an impression. It was somewhat like every atom in my body flying apart! I am speaking of the passage of time as measured out by Jesus. Time is a special ingredient when we actively surrender to it in an attitude of trust.

I am serious when I say that I knew time was a key factor in healing because were He to reach into our inner being and extract the hurt, pain, and self-protection we have so meticulously held in place, we would literally implode. There would be nothing left. We could not take all the pain that every trauma and hurt has caused us. Our walls have a purpose. God needs to create other support structures before tearing down the ones in place.

One of God's most incredible characteristics is patience. Many times, I have wept for the patience He has shown me. Patience is time on our side of eternity. We do not always cooperate with God's timetable, yet He patiently waits and presents the opportunity for healing to continue. He waits for our "yes," followed by an action that moves toward His heart. That action is trust, another word for faith.

The Lord's mind is far beyond our own. He knows that He will do more than heal our wounds. He will develop patience in us through our suffering. He will establish trust in Him and others as we proceed with healing. We will have greater character when we gain His patience. We will deal with others mercifully rather than wanting to hurl insults, curses, and take revenge.

On more than one occasion, I have wondered why my healing did not occur more rapidly once I had begun the initial process. Why couldn't I have continued the healing I received earlier in life? What was so special at age forty-three? I wish I had the answer. All I know is that everything that had happened prior to that age was preparation.

God is concerned for all things physical, spiritual, mental, and emotional in our lives. He alone understands the intricacies of how they fit together and what needs to be done so that all the planes of our lives work toward wholeness of our being.

Some of what I understand is that the Lord had been building trust from earlier healing. He healed my broken truster. The process no longer surprised me. He took away the dread of what might be next and created an expectancy of freedom that surpassed my fear of pain.

When I was younger, I thought Christians got to bypass emotional pain. What patience God spent to get me over that one misunderstanding! Neither did I give in to discouragement. In the beginning, it often felt devastating. At the time, I did not grasp how He changed my view from almost compulsive introspection and faultfinding to His truth. Introspection led me down a spiraling abyss of self-loathing. The truth led me to a healthy self-acceptance, even liking. What an incredible blessing that God knows us better than we know ourselves!

My sincere hope is that you understand more about forgiveness, forgiving, and the time it takes God to work these things in our lives. Nothing in this book is new. I have simply shared the experiences and affect the truth has had on my own heart and soul. I choose to act on it, get forgiveness, give forgiveness, and let the Lord bring healing to my torn soul in His time. I am grateful for the ministry others have provided in their writings on the healing of the soul. This offering is merely another testimony to the healing power of the gospel of Jesus

Christ. I pray that what I have presented may be used to bring clarity to you who read this.

We are each unique. Our journeys are different, the layers of wounding in different order. However, no matter the differences, God's truth about forgiveness, forgiving, and the time needed for His healing remain constant.

I want to revisit the analogy of the trapeze from Chapter Five for a moment. No one can escape God's requirement to turn loose of the earth's trapeze and grab hold of His spiritual one. We cannot receive healing by hanging on to both. We get nowhere fast. The trapezes originate from distinctly different realms. Most of us know the trapeze of our earthly experiences. We grab its miserable bar only because it is familiar.

A paradox of awful and pleasant things dangles from the bar to which we cling so tightly. It swings out over an open pit—with no safety nets below. Fear dangles beside and beneath us. The trapeze swings on and on. My, how tiresome and monotonous, but we must not let go; one quick glance down or to the side brings a rush of nauseating fear, so we cling, white-knuckled, ever tighter.

That goes on until we become conscious of another trapeze to grab onto. The new trapeze swings by. Someone on it offers me His hand. It is Jesus. Oh, how powerful His hand appears. He tells me my power will not hold me to His trapeze. He will hold me. He has everything I need to swing out over life. There are still pits below. I just noticed a ladder hanging on the bar of His trapeze. It will take concentrated effort to avoid falling, but I never saw anything before but the inevitable fall into the pit. He tells me that He used to be a carpenter and that He has the materials to build any bridge or make any ladder. How exciting to know a way has been provided over, through, or out of those precarious places.

Do I dare turn loose of my old trapeze and grab His hand? Yes, I think I will. "Oh, Jesus, there is a pit below, but I am not afraid. We will go over it together. The view beyond is the most beautiful thing I have ever seen. I want to stay on Your trapeze until it swings into eternity!"

Pardon my simple analogy, but I often use it to minister to someone about how to let go. Although my example is uncomplicated, what it represents is profound. Will you ask God to reveal the truth of this to you? Won't you let go of that trapeze that swings out over the abyss of fear and grab onto the hand of the One holding the trapeze that swings out over the land of blessing? God has even made provisions for pitfalls!

I know it is easy to tell you to reach out. It's letting go that is so difficult. If we do not release the old bar, we are stuck with no momentum in our fear and misery. The pain you have experienced does not define life. You are intended to live higher than the pit in which you dwell. God longs to exchange the narrow view of existence into which you have squeezed for His panoramic space. He waits to expand the limits that bind your perception. Listen to this wonderful promise in *1 Corinthians 2:9 (NIV)*: *"No eye has seen, no ear has heard, no mind has conceived what God prepared for those who love Him."* I invite you to believe this powerful truth. Won't you turn loose that miserable bar? Awesome wonders lie ahead.

Chapter Nine

Holes in Our Souls Need Maintaining

I believe that this chapter will be a bit of a surprise, but maybe not a total surprise. You see, I have a tendency to go on and on about Jesus. I just love Him. I never could have understood what that meant had He not loved me first. He has loved me just as I am at every stage of my life, and He loved me enough to not leave me as He found me. He promised *"that He who began a good work in you will carry it on to completion until the day of Jesus Christ." (Philippians 1:6 NIV)*

He did not leave me the shriveled soul that He found me. A few chapters ago, I told you I would finish the story about the terrible images that used to pop into my mind unexpectedly. They did not leave altogether until I was nineteen years old. Tormented dreams plagued me from age six to nineteen. They were especially egregious because they continued after my salvation experience.

My generation did not discuss some disturbing things, especially if you were a Christian. Social and spiritual limits did not permit me to unload what came, uninvited, to my mind; I had no way to understand the origin of the images. I assumed them to be part of be my own thoughts. I felt an awful burden of guilt. I felt ashamed and unworthy of forgiveness, even though I knew God had saved my soul. My misery mounted.

I did not learn about spiritual warfare until my late twenties. Then, I began to understand the kind of enemy I had and how effectively he, the devil, could work against me. After all, he had insider information. He watched my family's previous generations. He knew what traps to set to capture my soul. Secrets, verbal, physical, and sexual abuse, addictions, unfaithfulness, abandonment, adultery—my family album was full of images distorted by the evils of generational sin. The only thing my enemy had to do was devise snares based on the information he had gathered.

But my Heavenly Father made provision for me long before the devil ever baited his first hooks. He knew the hour, the day, the moment He would rescue me. Just as He had appointed the day for me to hear the gospel and become a believer, He set up the appointment for my release from my bondage over two thousand years ago.

That provision, the death, burial, and resurrection of His Son Jesus would save my life from eternal torment and be my deliverance from earthly torment. What a mind God has. We cannot fathom His plan.

His is a greater power than any plan, device, or snare of the enemy! The power of Jesus projects backward in time to every sin ever committed, and His power projects forward to retrieve the penalty of every present sin. His blood-bought power provides forgiveness for all future sin when I come to Him with a repentant heart. That power exists to heal broken souls and lives. I can't help but say, "Wow!"

Just as I can turn to pictures of myself in an album and see my physical changes, so I can turn back the pages of my soul and be profoundly affected by the changes I see in my mind, will, and emotions. I did not do the changing. It came by exposure to Jesus and His loving, persistent cutting out the messes of my life and super-gluing in the blessedness of His.

From the first pages of this book, I called Him the soul-maker, the One who designed every detail of our being. He is the master architect of the world, universe, and body, soul, and spirit. He is also the soul-healer, the doctor I told you about in Chapter One.

He earned that title by leaving His position as our soul-maker, and voluntarily enrolling in life's university and taking every course ever offered by man or structured by the devil. He passed every course and mastered each one. He is the only student who ever made a perfect grade in the school of life.

Upon graduation from this life, He earned a degree offered to no other, for no other has ever passed its qualifications before. He is the soul-healer. He is the Son of God, who chose to live within the constraints of humanity and exposed Himself to prideful contempt.

As the soul-healer, He can extract the puss of every evil. He can close any gaping wound because He is expert in performing the most exacting operations to kill the infections that exposure to sin has caused. For our deliverance, He exposed Himself to the unimaginable.

He did not inoculate Himself against the evils of this earth. He embraced the same experiences as you and I. He did not turn away from rejection, shame, betrayal, abuse, beatings, or even death. He did not run away, hide, protect Himself, or offer excuses. He claimed no exemption because He was God; He chose to suffer as a man.

He did not use His power as the Son of God. He lived surrendered to His Father's power. He relied on His Father's voice. He waited on His Father's command as to when to release His power. He endured every hurt and did not seek revenge. He kept silent when accused falsely. He offered up His perfect life to the imperfect and gravely flawed judgments of human authorities. This is just a hint of what He went through to become the soul-healer.

I know that these things have been stated a little differently in previous chapters, but I wanted to reiterate them once more before telling you the rest of my story. I did not know until I began writing this chapter what God would have me put into its contents. Interestingly, it was written after the last chapter of this book was complete.

I needed to revisit a subject requiring its own space. Part of my testimony concerns the soul-healer's tender care and enduring patience. Pieces of my story highlight His awesome knowledge of what to do and when to do it. His wisdom bears the fruit of meaning and purpose. In all the years of ministering to other hurting people, I have found the particular soul wound that seemingly takes the most profound healing—sexual molestation. The affects are evidenced in every layer of the being. It takes a great amount of time, patience, and processing to heal. Above all, it requires the supernatural work of God done by His Son on the cross to mend the damages. He does the maintenance needed afterward through the indwelling of His Holy Spirit.

Sexual molestation in all its forms, from incest to rape, tears the fragile fabric of one's inner self; it perverts the mind's understanding of love and the emotions' responses. It leaves the soul with broken gates and mile-high walls. It captures innocence, pronounces endings before beginnings, redefines hope as hopeless, and makes every attempt to turn lies into truth. Its filth mars all that is clean. Control comes as intimidation and the intimidator. Life becomes a never-ending battle to remain sane and keep inner pain sedated. Identity becomes skewed and pretense is often preferred over reality. Victims become victimizers—on and on.

But I think the most horrendous thing it accomplishes is the distortion of our view of God. That one target causes diabolical joy in hell and claims of victory by the devil. He throws accusatory questions such as, "Where was God when this happened?" into the mixture of plaguing doubts about God's love. "After all," he mercilessly interjects into our minds, "God did not prevent this evil from happening."

Not one time does he dare let the light of truth into thoughts that victims take as their own. He keeps the blame foremost so that the victim does not understand that the devil is the one at work. He works feverishly to hide the truth that a different life is available to be lived.

That misery was my existence—first in the torment of my mind as a little girl. The images that appeared in my mind were too awful to expose to anyone. I had a dream about being in a terrible place, strapped down, my private parts being touched. Fear that someone would know about the terrible images locked me in a prison of silence and self-loathing. It thrust me into trying to do enough good to override the awfulness inside my mind.

I did not know what had happened to me until my early forties. In the late 1980s and 90s, several programs about molestation aired on television. As I watched, I realized that a few of the characteristic behaviors of molested individuals discussed on those shows seemed descriptive of me.

During my second marriage, God began to reveal many of the behaviors and attitudes that matched those molestation victims. I tried to deny the truth because I had no memory of anything happening to me. I just knew that in intimate moments, I would often curl into a fetal position, lock up inside, jump at the slightest touch, and begin to shake uncontrollably. I began to loathe sex. I did not understand my responses, because that had not happened in my earlier marriage. However, in my first marriage, I initiated intimacy most of the time, which happened less and less as the years passed. My first husband cared more for me as a friend than a wife.

Later, I grasped that as long as I was the pursuer of intimacy, the hidden memory of molestation lay dormant. Once I married a man who loved me and desired physical intimacy that which was hidden came to life like an inactive volcano that suddenly began to rumble and then violently erupted.

God gave me an incredible man in my second marriage. My torment not only affected me, but him. Besides the physical responses that emerged, so did toxic and bitter attitudes toward men. I often railed at him in unbridled anger. I believe God gave my husband an added measure of His divine love for me. With Garry's patient faithfulness, we stayed the difficult course of God's healing in my life.

None of the exposed attitudes and behaviors agreed with what I knew and believed as a Christian. I knew God meant for men to be loving protectors, but my heart rejected that truth. The constant tug of war between my head and heart made me feel I was going crazy, but because of how the Lord watched over me through the years, maintained my growth as a Christian, and revealed pertinent information at just the right time, I accepted the truth. I asked Him to end my internal tug of war. I wanted His truth in both places! He did just that.

A step at a time, He brought me from the dark prison of my soul, where I sat on the icy floor, arms wrapped tightly about my knees, my exhausted body rocking back and forth, my distraught mind so full of excruciating pain I did not even dare to think. For the first time, I chose to respond to the call I heard outside the door. I recognized the voice. It was the same voice I heard call me to salvation at age eleven. Jesus! He told me to get up from the icy floor. I placed my shaking hands on the lock, turned it, opened the door, and let Him in. I stood there as the warmth of His loving presence and truth engulfed me. He loosed my shackles of self-hatred, shame, torment, fears, rejection, and generational sin. He brought peace to my troubled mind and renewed it with His truth until it dropped into my heart. I began to be transformed from a little half-orphaned girl wandering aimlessly around to the daughter of the Lord, a royal heir able to plug into to every promise of God. My sad countenance changed. I took off my spirit of heaviness and put on a new garment of praise. He anointed me with the oil of joy, just as He had promised in *Isaiah 61*.

If reality is as simple as "God is only good" and "the devil is only evil," it means that the two are mutually exclusive. God cannot but do good, and the devil cannot but do evil. If God is only good, then He can make a way out. He can deliver us from misery, as we believe in His Word that He comes to set the captives free. He is the way-maker, but He waits for our invitation because from the beginning, God gave every man and woman free will instead of making us robots.

To allow us to have that free will, God had to allow Satan's rebellion in heaven to fall to a place, a realm, and a sphere of influence. That place was planet Earth. But Satan had no power to rule over man until man gave him power through his own choosing.

Sin came to life when Satan's bait was taken: the desire to be like God was chosen over walking with Almighty God every day in the Garden of Eden. Man and woman had a choice, and they both chose sin. From that first moment, sin's way has been the way of destruction and death. Ages before Eve ate and offered her husband the first tempting bite of forbidden fruit, God had His plan for man's redemption set up.

Satan did not take God by surprise, although he did surprise mankind with his half-truths and convincing lies. Truth is the essence of God, and it sets us free. Satan wanted to destroy relationship with God through disobedience. But God would not just be truth, He would birth truth to destroy Satan's works and evil plans. His only Son, Jesus, came to earth with the power to set us free, gain an eternal relationship with God, and to secure abundant life for us here on earth. When Jesus returned to Heaven, He released the Holy Spirit.

When we yield to the Holy Spirit's control, He maintains our faith, our life, our direction, and our growth as a follower of Jesus. He brings God's Word to life, gives understanding of spiritual things, and convicts our hearts of sin. He also gives us gifts to use to help others come to know God's great love and plan for their lives. He leads us to what we need to pray and know. He increases our sense of God's presence and God's call to His service.

In addition, The Spirit renews us and works to restore us from the inside out; He enables us to discern between soul and spirit. He prompts us to prayer, petition, and thanksgiving. He makes us to know the difference between true goodness and disguised evil. He reveals things God wants us to know to our innermost being.

Sometimes, I recall how I used to respond to so many things in a negative way, and I have to pinch myself to realize how differently I view things now. It doesn't mean that I always feel positive. I don't. The difference is that I understand that there is a choice. If I make a positive choice against the negative way I feel and yield to the Holy Spirit, my feelings will change and be in line with God's.

He is God's barometer who lives in my spirit. If I let Him direct, or redirect my choices through surrendered prayer, I emerge in peace, not consternation. My decisions are not "if-y" but confident. The maintainer of my soul leads me in wisdom toward a life of peace, regardless of the tumultuousness around me.

God's program for my life is always available. Accessibility is dependent upon trading my way for His, forgiving those who offend me, accepting His righteousness in place of mine, and receiving His truth into my being. I've surrendered to it enough to know that I don't ever want to live without it. The maintenance program has no unseen fees or hidden clauses. It is renewable for life.

I know of nothing I recommend more than God's maintenance agreement. You get it at no charge by asking His beloved Son to take control at the seat of your being. He will come to dwell there by the power of the Holy Spirit. You, too, will receive access to a life of the greatest peace, healing, and stability you have ever known. It never runs out, either. Want it? You can have it. Remember, it is free for the asking!

Chapter Ten

Holes in Our Souls Have Purpose

*I*t is a pleasure to be at this point in our journey together. If you dare to put the foot of faith to what has been shared, you will discover that when Jesus heals our souls by the revelation and power of the Holy Spirit, the healed holes have tremendous purpose. We have not been ripped and torn for nothing, unless we choose for it to remain that way.

Scars do not represent random hunks of pain that resign us to the waste bin of existence. They are reservoirs of God's glorious truth, meant to flow to other needy captives of hurt and pain. They become awesome witnesses to the power of the gospel of Jesus Christ.

Jesus is not a voyeur to the healing of the soul. He experienced every type of wound known to man, including unjustified death. The One who authored life and raised the dead was falsely accused repeatedly. Further, following a long night of soul-tugging prayer that resulted in the blood sweating choice of "yes", He willingly submitted to His accusers, who voted to crucify Him.

He loved His accusers even as they shouted mocking hatred and raised angry fists in unison with their cries of "Kill Him!" He did not submit because He loved those present at the time, but because He was looking across all time, into the evil effect of sin in the lives of mankind with that same love.

He went a step further. He took on all the sin of man from the first tick of time until the last tock of time. It is nearly impossible to comprehend this kind of love. Is it any wonder that such love holds an incomprehensible power? It changes hearts, lives, families, cities, states, provinces, regions, and nations!

Recall with me that He never sinned. Never did He have an evil, mean, or vengeful thought. Never did He talk disrespectfully to His parents. He did not fight with His brothers or those who poked fun at His obedient ways and called Him a goody two-shoes. He kept God's every commandment perfectly every minute, every hour, and every single day of His thirty-three-year life.

He had no pride, jealousy, or envy. He did not lust in His mind or body during the turbulent years of puberty. He was patient in every trial, temperate, peaceful in word and action, kind to friend and foe, gentle in nature, good from the inside out, meek, loving in every painful situation, and joyful in impossible circumstances.

He was also a man of sorrows, well acquainted with grief according to *Isaiah 53:3.* Because He was also God, He not only knew His but ours. According to *verses 4 and 5* of *Isaiah 53,* He took our infirmities and carried our sorrows. Who He was, and what He did made Him God's healer. He was *"pierced for our transgressions, He was crushed for our iniquities; the punishment that brought us peace was upon Him and by His wounds we are healed."*

We go to human doctors who study every kind of disease. They are full of knowledge about diseases they may have never experienced. They can give advice and prescribe medications, but more times than not, they have little knowledge of the ravages of the disease in their own bodies. Doctor Jesus is not like that. He is the doctor of all doctors, the healer who specializes in "internal medicine" of the body, the mind, and emotions.

Hebrews 4:15 helps us understand why Jesus chose to experience all that He did for us: *"For we do not have a high priest who is unable to sympathize with our weaknesses, but we have One who has been tempted in every way, just as we are-yet without sin." (NIV)* He wanted to be the One who understands us so much that He could present us to His Father, and say, "I will suffer every kind of pain and suffering that they do, that I may indeed heal every part of them: body, soul, and spirit."

We are further encouraged because of what Jesus did in his suffering. He approached the throne of God's grace with confidence, having suffered without sin so that we could go to that same throne. We receive mercy and find grace in our time of our need. His throne is the zone to which we can run for results.

Human shackles leave evidence of our captivity. Our healed souls bear witness to a greater body of evidence. They are testimonies to what is no more! There is no shame—only thanksgiving for the freedom. We look inside, and instead of torment, we find peace. Where degradation ruled, honor prevails. Where meanness dominated, kindness reigns.

I cannot help sounding enthusiastic. This is the basis of my own testimony. Doctor Jesus made several personal visits to the house of my wounded soul, and lovingly, tenderly, and persistently took the diseased substances out of me. He applied the balm of His healing truth mixed with forgiveness and mercy. The results are the skin I live in daily. There are marked differences from my once offensive behaviors, which were the reflections of infections from sin's deadly works.

It doesn't matter where the source of sin comes from. The same results manifest for me and all of mankind—death. Death of important relationships, death of significant fellowship, death of healthy desires and goals, death of strength, and eventually, physical death. It kills the body, torments the mind, bends the will toward unhealthy actions, and incapacitates goodly behaviors.

For many years, I was an abandoned, dejected, and rejected soul. I could not believe that anyone would really want to be me with on a permanent basis. That lie allowed many other self-deprecating, self-rejecting untruths to hold my inner being in captivity for too long.

I don't play those videos in my mind and heart anymore because I have been delivered from the sin, unforgiveness, hurt, and wounding. The star in my life's movies now is my beloved Savior, champion, and hero—Jesus! Many of the same subjects are on display, but the endings have been re-written. Instead of defeat, there is victory. No more shame, just a lot of thanksgiving. I am no longer the victim but the victor.

The soul that chooses to let Jesus heal it becomes a poster boy or girl for God's splendor, life, and healing. They offer hope to a hopeless world. They pass out more than a band-aid. Their scars reflect light and life, not darkness, torment, and heaviness. No bitterness seeps from cracked, broken emotions because it has been eradicated. The emotions and memories receive lasting healing. Life can progress.

Through Christ's work on the cross, emotions that leapt from past woundings into the present detach into the past without rancor, revenge, hatred, or revulsion. We can release the things of the past without adopting a new set of coping skills or taking pills that disguise what is pushed beneath the surface. When someone tells me that he or she is over something painful from the past through a new "fix", I find that, the "fix" becomes the new subject. That is, until the fix is no longer sufficient.

Please do not think that I do not believe in the help offered by doctors or therapy and counseling. I absolutely do. However, man-made solutions are temporary helps. Man is limited, but God is limitless. They have their place and time. God may use them throughout our lives. Once medical professionals and their treatments accomplish their goal, we need help of a more permanent nature. That more permanent help exists in the wholeness and completeness of God Almighty.

The work of the cross is love, the earth-bound God-man doing what we could never do for ourselves: overcoming sin—

its temptations, effects, torment, and penalties. According to God's Word in *1 Corinthians 13:8, "Love never fails."* He desires His love to transform our lives, so that we turn share His love with a wounded world.

My desire is for you to have the endings to your life's movies rewritten, as mine and many others I know have been. There is a standing invitation from the Author of Life to whoever will take it. Won't you make an appointment soon? His schedule is open. When He is finished redirecting your history, He wants to publish it through the works of your hands. The world needs what He has done in you to be on display.

We do not become little saviors; we become walking signposts of The Savior who lives inside us. Hope, life, grace, and peace reside in our beings as we go through the struggles of existence. Oh, yes, struggles go on even as healing continues and wholeness ripens. At sixty, I have experienced many ups and downs. God never erased the inevitable difficulties. He just made the way through them.

The light of the eternal breaks in on the horizons of our temporal experiences, and we are changed. I have been greatly healed and tempered by His continuing work. I expect even bigger results as I look forward to the years ahead.

May God bless each of you, wherever you are in your journey, whether you are just accepting His invitation, or you are down the road apiece. May your life's story be one of God's transformational masterpieces that offer hope to the hopeless. May your road lead from victory to victory, and your countenance shine with the beauty of new beginnings. May your heart reflect the healing touch of Jesus that reaches out to others who need this truth displayed: God restores the broken and sets the captives free. May you go on from glory to glory, claiming meaning and showcasing the purposes for which you were born!

End Notes and Questions

An observation I made during my soul's healing is that the use of questions has often been instrumental in unlocking doors of revelation. I know I will never forget the afternoon my friend and partner in ministry asked me a non-judgmental, provoking question that unlocked the door of lies that imprisoned the real me. Her question was God's way out for me into truth and greater freedom than I had known.

Following these endnotes, I want you to peruse some questions and answer the ones that God is shining His light on for your revelation. The question section that follows is only meant to be a help. As you read this book, many of you paused and prayed at the various places. Some of you have found life in God through His Son for the first time. You have also entered the process of the healing and transforming your soul. May you be as greatly blessed as you begin your journey as I continue to be on mine.

Others have known salvation for a long time. Perhaps you have been on the road of healing from your soul's wounds, and God used this to give you understanding for just where you are or where He is leading you. I encourage you to move each time He brings you revelation.

Still others picked this book up out of curiosity, read it, and are still questioning its validity. I pray that your curiosity has been provoked to test the truth presented. The truth is never complex. It is simple. Humans make it complicated. As I formerly stated, that does not mean the process is easy. God wanted everyone to understand how to know Him and how to be healed by Him.

I am thankful to all those God has used to help me in my journey of His salvation and soul healing. He made us unique. Many others who wrote of the way God used their unique blends of personality, experience, gifts, talents, and faith have helped me. Some of God's teachers and exhorters in my life are from other centuries; some are alive today.

My personality and gifts do not display great intellect, but I do have the products of a sifted heart that sees simply, by the working grace of God and His great love. That love encompasses a majestic plan for us all, no matter our heredity or environmental influences. It can touch our frayed past, our overwhelming present, or our deepest longings of tomorrow.

If anything offered in this book has helped you in any way, then its purpose has been accomplished. As you look through the questions that follow, I pray you will be directed toward an answer you may be seeking. They are intended to lead you straight to the doctor who heals completely, patiently, and with expertise and compassion. I know you know His name by now—Jesus!

In hope, prayer, and faith for God's healing in your life,

Sharon L. Patterson

Questions

Chapter One: Holes in Our Souls Are Common To Us All

1. Are any past situations with former bosses or co-workers as fresh in your memory today as the day they took place?

2. What kind of hole in your soul did that situation leave with you? (Example: betrayal)

3. Have any holes emerged concerning friendships? What hole has it left? (Example: distrust)

4. What about family relationships? (Really sticky. I know.)

5. Who helped you deal with some of these situations, and how were you helped?

6. Have you experienced trauma at any time in your life that plagues you in any way today? Have you gone for help when the resulting feelings seemed overwhelming?

7. Have "familiar places of misery" been preferable places at times in your life?

8. What stirs you to move past the familiar places?

9. What are some of the things you have used to cover the holes in your soul?

10. What is your relationship to God like? Would you like it to be different? How?

Questions

Chapter Two: Holes in Our Souls
Happen Through Heredity and Environment

1. Have you ever been compared to someone in your family?

2. What was the comparison about?

3. Concerning your family, what are some traits that you definitely have? (Be sure to list the positive ones as well!)

4. What is your response to the information about dysfunctional families and their stories in the Bible?

5. What is your response to the verse from *Jeremiah 29:11* concerning God's plans for you? Is it hard to believe? What prevents you from believing it?

6. Are there times that you know your life has been preserved in trouble? *(Psalm 138:7)* Does it bring you comfort to recall these?

7. Who has been a part of the healing you have already received? Have you been able to extend gratitude that you feel toward the person(s) that have helped you?

8. When you have uncomfortable feelings that bring anxiety, how do you find comfort? What is the result? Comfort or further discomfort?

9. Do you ever feel guilty over irrational behaviors with others in situations that make you uncomfortable? What do you do with that guilt?

10. What wounds have come from the environment in which you were raised? Which have come from family?

11. What are some areas in which you know you are healed?

12. What proves that to you?

13. How do you feel God has directed your healing?

14. Has this chapter brought any new considerations for you in the area of faith, prayer, or the Bible?

15. Is there any step in the healing process that has become clearer to you?

Questions

Chapter Three: Holes in Our Souls
Contain Toxic and Infectious Substances

1. Do you accept God's Word as the source of truth?

2. How is knowing truth and acting on truth different concerning the healing of our inner being?

3. After reading the scripture from *Isaiah 61:1-4,* what things on the list seem to speak to you most?

4. Go ahead and list the things that excited your heart on page 16, even if it is hard to believe yet.

5. Are there things that you identify with on page 20? Please list those that are no longer operative in your life.

6. What things from that list are still active in your life?

7. What are your desires from the revised list on pages 21 and 22?

8. Who can destroy the evil work done to our souls, according to *1 John 3:8?*

9. How do you feel about giving God the house of your soul with all that is good and all that is bad?

10. Have you ever taken God's trade-in? Your life for His? Would you like to if you haven't? A prayer for the trade-in is found on page 25.

Questions

Chapter Four: Holes in Our Souls Need Healing

1. What are some temporary camouflages you have used to cover holes in your soul?

2. What happens when we do not tend to the holes in our souls?

3. What oozes from the holes in your soul? Does anything mentioned in the fourth paragraph on page 28 seem familiar in your life?

4. What part has insecurity played in your life? Is this a new consideration for you?

5. What has been your journey in seeking help for the hurting places inside?

6. Can you name what has particularly drawn your attention along the way?

7. What has been the result of the things you have tried?

8. Have you ever had someone speak the truth to you at a time you could not receive it?

9. What is the difference when you know that you have received truth directly to your spirit?

10. Who makes us to know what truth is?

11. Can you describe salvation as presented in this chapter in your own words?

12. What does it mean to be a new creation? *(2 Corinthians 5:17)*

13. How do I appropriate that truth if I have made the trade-in of God's life for mine?

14. Why is it necessary to unlearn things we once felt were true because of life's experiences? (Example: "I am not worthy; I'm no good because I am damaged.")

15. How do I learn to recognize truth?

16. Who is the Holy Spirit?

17. What are His functions in the life of a believer?

18. Why doesn't God simply touch us and heal us instantly?

19. How is lost trust rebuilt?

20. What is the difference in introspection and God's inward searching of our soul? How are the results different?

Questions

Chapter Five: Holes in Our Souls Need Uncovering

1. Why must the holes in our souls be uncovered?

2. Why does God allow scabs to grow over some of the wounds in our lives?

3. How do you think self-loathing and self-pity block our view of truth?

4. With what things from my story can you identify?

5. Why do you think God delays giving us the answers we ask for?

6. Why would God give us a "no" to an answer?

7. Why would God allow us to go through painful experiences to lead us to healing?

8. Has your identity ever been tied to what you do?

9. What has been your revelatory moment to come out of bondage from hurt? How did it happen?

10. Talk about any restoration experiences that have occurred in your life following healing from wounds to your soul.

11. Did you receive any light concerning any places inside that you recognize need to be uncovered?

12. Are you ready to give God your fear to "go there?" Revisit page 48.

Questions

Chapter Six: Holes in Our Souls Need Lancing

1. Why is it necessary to lance our soul's wounds?

2. How did the description of lancing in this chapter help you to understand this need?

3. How can we guard against re-infection after we experience the lancing of a soul wound?

4. Will God force me to have my wound lanced?

5. Do I only get one chance to have my wound lanced? What happens if I quit before it is done?

6. Can I bypass this step in healing?

7. How can a lancing be bittersweet?

8. Who does God use as assistants in the lancing of our soul's wounds? What types of ministry does He use?

9. What wounds have you knowingly had lanced by the Lord?

10. Have you had revelation of a wound yet to be lanced? Were you encouraged about the heart of the One who does the lancing?

Questions

Chapter Seven: Holes in Our Souls Need Filling

1. What is the promise of Jeremiah 30:17?

2. What is the medicine of God?

3. What is the main cause of wounding?

4. To what kind of wounding was Jesus exposed?

5. Are there any mentioned that have happened to you?

6. Why did Jesus become the medicine of God?

7. How did He become the medicine of God?

8. Is there anything new you discovered in reading the passage from Isaiah on page 61?

9. What was God's purpose in allowing His Son to suffer for all mankind? (Hint: last line of *Isaiah 53*)

10. Are there things that happened in my story that have happened in yours? Are you encouraged about how the medicine of God healed my wounds?

Questions

Chapter Eight: Holes in Our Souls
Need Forgiveness, Forgiving, and Time

1. Have you been a victim? Of what?

2. Have you been a victimizer?

3. Why is it necessary to forgive?

4. What will happen if I don't forgive?

5. Why is it necessary to be in the receiving mode as well as the giving mode concerning forgiveness?

6. Why compare unforgiveness to cancer?

7. How do we get the hallway of forgiveness installed in the house of our inner being?

8. How do I keep that hallway clear?

9. What part does time play in the forgiveness process?

10. Why doesn't God heal us of all our wounds at once, or at least in rapid succession?

11. Is there ever an injustice I will not be required to forgive? Why is it worth it to let go of every bit of unforgiveness? (Hint: *1 Corinthians 2:9*)

12. When I say "forgiveness," does anyone come to mind?

13. Are there any offenses in your hallway that need clearing?

14. Is there anything you hold against yourself?

15. Write forgiven across this page when you are finished!

Questions

Chapter Nine: Holes in Our Souls Need Maintaining

1. What hope about healing is offered in *Philippians1:6?*

2. Why do the holes in our souls need maintaining?

3. Are we alone in the things we must do to maintain our healing?

4. What is God's provision in the maintaining of our soul's health?

5. How does knowing all that Jesus has done build confidence in what He will do?

6. Can Jesus really heal the wounds that come from molestation, whether from a family member, friend, or stranger?

7. What are the wounds that are the most difficult to "get over"?

8. Why are these wounds particularly devastating?

9. If God is truly good, how can He let devastating things happen?

10. Describe God's maintenance program. Do I have to get a new maintenance agreement once I have used it?

Questions

Chapter Ten: Holes in Our Souls Have Purpose

1. How do scars of suffering become healing reservoirs of God's truth about freedom to others?

2. How can we understand this from the life of Jesus, our healer?

3. For a wonderful reminder, go to page 84 and write *Isaiah 53:5* at the bottom of the page.

4. We know why God let His Son suffer, but why did Jesus say, "Yes"? (Hint: *Hebrews 4:15*)

5. What rights did Jesus gain for us?

6. If the results of sin lead to death of relationships, strength, and vitality of life, what are some of the gains of healing?

7. How can we tell the story of what has happened to us without shame coming along for the ride?

8. Finish this statement about the benefits of healing: "I am no longer the victim, but the_____!" Is this a statement you feel you can make because of prayers and decisions you made after reading *Healing for the Holes in Our Souls*? Please write what you know has changed inside.

9. How can life progress when we get healing from our soul's wounds?

10. What does God want to display to the world about His healing? Who gets to be His poster children?

Works of Others God Has Used in My Life

I wanted to include a list of the works that the Lord has used in my life during His healing process. They offered me hope and gave me understanding at significant moments. They helped me when I was stuck, and spurred me to move on with God. I still go back to some of these for their evidence and witness of the awesome power of the gospel of Jesus Christ.

My heart is forever grateful that God has given special insight through His servants as they have gone through their transformations and understandings. If I were to include every influence, this list would be longer than my book. Here are a few of the ones of which I am most appreciative. I have given credit for the inspiration they invoked in my life.

INSPIRATION TO UNDERSTAND

Nine O' Clock in the Morning by Dennis J. Bennett

Pigs in the Parlor by Frank and Ida Mae Hammond

They Shall Expel Demons by Derek Prince

They Speak with Other Tongues by Jack Hayford

The Transformation of the Inner Man by John Sandford

Latent Power of the Soul by Watchman Nee

INSPIRATION TO GROW

Hinds' Feet on High Places by Hannah Hurnard

My Utmost for His Highest by Oswald Chambers

Abide In Christ by Andrew Murray

God Calling by A.J. Russell

Breaking Free by Beth Moore (as well as many of her Bible Studies)

Various biographies and autobiographies of God's leaders in other centuries are listed in "A Special Footnote"

INSPIRATION TO HEAL

Light in My Darkest Night by Catherine Marshall

The Hiding Place by Corrie ten Boom

Healing the Wounded Spirit by John and Paula Sandford

When God Weeps by Joni Eareckson Tada

When the Night Is Too Long by Robert L. Wise

Toxic Faith by Stephen Arterburn and Jack Felton

Restoring the Christian Soul by Leanne Payne

Listening Prayer by Leanne Payne

Freeing Your Mind from Memories that Bind by Fred and Florence Littauer

INSPIRATION TO MINISTER

The Spirit-Controlled Temperament by Tim LaHaye

The Personality Tree by Florence Littauer

The Bondage Breaker by Neil T. Anderson

Transforming the Inner Man by John Loren and Paula Sandford

Battlefield of the Mind by Joyce Meyer

Managing Your Emotions by Joyce Meyer

The Purpose Driven Life by Rick Warren

Just Give Me Jesus by Anne Graham Lotz

INSPIRATION TO ENJOY

This Present Darkness by Frank Peretti

Piercing the Darkness by Frank Peretti

Redeeming Love by Francine Rivers

A Voice in the Wind by Francine Rivers

Echo in the Darkness by Francine Rivers

Sure Dawn by Francine Rivers

In The Grip of Grace by Max Lucado

A Place to Call Home by Deborah Smith

The Divine Romance by Gene Edwards

Israel My Beloved by Kay Arthur

The Mitford Years and other series by Jan Karon

The Left Behind Series by Tim LaHaye and Jerry Jenkins

A Special Footnote

There have been many influences on the healing of my wounded soul and on my growth and development as a Christian. I have always been fascinated with the works and biographies of Christians throughout the ages. I wanted to include a special list of a few of the lives that have given me inspiration through their stories of courage, boldness, and destiny for the times to which they were born. .

SIXTEENTH CENTURY

John Foxe (1516-1587) Wrote *Foxe's Book of Martyrs,* which was put into every church, meeting hall, and college in England in Queen Elizabeth I's reign

SEVENTEENTH CENTURY

John Milton (1608-1674) Blind author of *Paradise Lost*

John Bunyan (1628-1688) Author of *Pilgrim's Progress* . Imprisoned for twelve years.

Madame Jeanne Guyon (1647-1717) Christian author who was persecuted and imprisoned under the reign of Louis XIV

EIGHTEENTH CENTURY (PLUS)

Jonathan Edwards (1703-1758) American theologian

John Wesley (1703-1791) Anglican minister who founded the Methodist Movement

George Whitfield (1714-1770) Evangelist who preached in England and America to crowds so large he was forced to preach outdoors

Charles Finney (1792-1875) Lawyer turned evangelist who fathered modern evangelism

NINETEENTH CENTURY (PLUS)

Hudson Taylor (1832-1905) Christian missionary to China

George Mueller (1805-1898) Founded movement establishing orphanages, relying greatly on prayer and faith

Dwight L. Moody (1837-1899) Great evangelistic outreach in America and

England

Andrew Murray (1828-1917) Author of *Absolute Surrender*

Oswald Chambers (1874-1917) Author of popular spiritual devotional *My Utmost for His Highest*

TWENTIETH/TWENTY-FIRST CENTURIES

Billy Sunday (1862-1935) Baseball athlete turned evangelist

Amy Carmichael (1867-1951) Irish missionary to India who rescued many young Indian girls in need

Corrie ten Boom (1892-1983) Author of *The Hiding Place,* the incredible autobiography of her imprisonment at Ravensbruck, Germany for hiding Jews during World War II

Watchman Nee (1903-1972) Authored many books during his twenty-year imprisonment in China, such as *Latent Power of the Soul, Normal Christian Life,* and *Changed into His Likeness*

Mother Teresa (1919-1997) Nun who founded Missionaries of Charity and won the Nobel Peace Prize in 1979 for her work in Calcutta

Billy Graham (1918-) Greatest American evangelist of the 20th Century

Made in the USA
Coppell, TX
24 June 2021